THE SOVIET CIRCUS

A SERIES OF ARTICLES

**Compiled
by**

Alexander Lipovsky

Fredonia Books
Amsterdam, The Netherlands

The Soviet Circus:
A Series of Articles

Compiled by
Alexander Lipovsky

ISBN: 1-58963-970-7

Reprinted from the 1967 edition

Fredonia Books
Amsterdam, The Netherlands
http://www.fredoniabooks.com

CONTENTS

AN AMAZING ART

By Herman Titov

The Circus. This word has always evoked in me a feeling of awe for the daredevil aerialists, the astounding acrobats, the funny clowns and the fearless animal-trainers.

As is usually the case, I fell in love with the circus when I was still a little boy. There was no circus in my native Altai, but this did not stop my friends and me from playing circus. Actually, I was drafted into being a gymnast. One day when I was riding my bicycle I fell and hurt my hand rather badly. The doctor said that the only hope of regaining the use of my fingers was in exercise. Thus my regular training began, and soon I was as keen on gymnastics as I was on riding my bicycle.

It is good to know that nowadays stars of the Soviet circus often tour the small towns and villages, making thousands upon thousands of new friends.

I was an aviation cadet when I first saw a real circus performance and was fascinated by this wonderful world of movement, colour, light and music. From then on I became a real circus fan.

The air regiment I served in paid special attention to physical training, for modern planes need flyers that are physically fit and can endure great strain. The flyers worked out in the gym and many took up acrobatics. Two of my friends and I set up our own act which we called "The Ringside Acrobats." We performed at the regimental club and at the local bread-baking plant. Needless to say, we had a long way to go to compete with professional acrobats (and no doubt we would never have passed the entrance exams of any circus school), but our audiences gave us a warm reception.

* * *

This general physical health and my training in gymnastics and acrobatics were of great help in one of my most difficult exams, passing the medical committee prior to being enrolled in cosmonaut school. We spent many long hours working out in a large fully equipped sports area in our special training school while preparing for future flights. Besides, we also worked out on the trampoline.

This training instilled in me an even greater respect for the stars of the circus arena, for it revealed aspects of their amazing art that are usually unknown to circus audiences. I recall that when I first approached the trampoline I said to myself: "This will be fun. I've seen circus acrobats jumping up and down on it like rubber balls, doing somersaults and other tricks. All you have to do is to push off, the net will throw you up, and then all you do is keep turning."

But it was all quite different than I had imagined. My first time on the trampoline, I couldn't even do the simplest exercise. I realised then that this called for skill and the ability to control every muscle, something that could only be achieved after intensive training, for the facility with which the various tricks are done is the result of strenuous daily practice.

* * *

In the past few months I have met and talked with circus performers on several occasions. I spent many pleasant hours with them in far-off Djakarta, where a group of Soviet circus performers were on tour. I spoke with other stars in Moscow, after the preview performance of "Our First Encounter."

"Come and take part in the trapeze act," they suggested in jest.

5

"Oh, no, your work is too dangerous," I replied in like manner. "We cosmonauts have more reliable equipment."

This is truly so, for in the circus all the acts are based on the physical capacities of the performers and less so on the various mechanical devices which serve to demonstrate their skill, strength and endurance. A. V. Lunacharsky once said that the circus was "an extremely truthful example of human strength and skill."

I recently came upon a cartoon of a circus performance on the Moon. That was a peep into the future, if I may say so. Meanwhile, however, I find great pleasure, as do so many thousands of Soviet people, in spending a few free hours at the circus, admiring the skill of those who carry on this ever young, vital and amazing art.

1962

STARS OF THE SOVIET CIRCUS

The Durov name has been appearing on circus billboards for over half a century.

The Durovs, outstanding satirists and clowns, talented naturalists, animal-trainers and public figures, have put great effort into establishing the Russian circus as a true art form. They were innovators who were for ever seeking new forins of expression and new themes for their acts. They wanted the circus to be not only entertaining, but educational as well.

Vladimir and Anatoly Durov were the first of the clan to become famous as circus entertainers. They were truly great artists in their field.

Born of an old noble family, they broke with it to join a travelling troupe. The life they led was difficult and full of humiliation until they reached the top. In the beginning, as they stood on the small stages of fairground booths, listening to the noise of the market crowds, travelling from city to city in third-class carriages or tramping the dusty roads, the brothers came to know their people. They adopted the bantering folk manner that had its inception centuries ago in the buffoonery of the Russian fairground jesters, dressing wisdom in the vestments of the simpleton or fool. A clown entertaining the crowds with nonsense was

Vladimir Durov

At a word from him, the animals came to life, showing

certainly not a person to be taken seriously. Yet this clown discussed the state of affairs in tsarist Russia in a manner that would surely have been censored had it appeared in the newspapers or magazines. Most important, the clown's words were understandable to the masses. He expressed their thoughts and emotions and did it in a funny, fascinating way. There was reason to be delighted and to respect the clown.

Anatoly was a good acrobat, a magician and a wonderful reciter of monologues. Vladimir performed as an artist, doing instant sketches. He was also a magician and a strong man and sang ditties. Animals were gradually introduced into the act, and at first they served chiefly to intensify the humour of the pointed jokes.

This is the knowledge and skill the Durovs brought to the circus, winning national acclaim within a short time.

By the 1890s they had evolved the basic pattern of their classical act. Uniformed attendants parted ranks as the Durovs made their grand entrance. They circled round the arena, heads high, greeting the applauding audience by raising their bent arms. King of jesters, but never the king's jester! The jester of His Majesty the People!

a real sense of responsibility, hospitality,

the ability to express one's feelings

and to conceal them at social functions

Then, taking a stand at the arena entrance, Anatoly Durov would recite a topical satirical monologue. There followed a parade of trained animals, interspersed with jests and commentary.

Until now we have been speaking of both Durov brothers, and this is only natural, for both began their careers in the circus at the same time and both, though they appeared in different circuses, strived to establish the principles of clowning which are today known as "the Durov method."

11

Both Durovs were very talented performers, both were truly creative artists. As time went on it became apparent that Anatoly Durov had chosen satire as his field. Words became his major weapon; he liked to recite fables in the arena, pointing up their subtler meanings, stressing the idea behind each. The various animals in his act were always of secondary importance, appearing to illustrate, stress, or add a circus flavour to his puns. He was a clown and satirist, a pamphleteer appearing with performing animals.

Anatoly Durov died on January 8, 1916.

Vladimir Durov conversed with his audiences, sharing with them the wisdom of the folk story-teller. His patient training produced amazing results, and his performing animals put on skits such as the famous "Railway Station," in which all the parts are played by animals.

Vladimir Durov enlarged his animal troupe to include an elephant, seals and other rare and interesting animals. But his major achievement in this field was his radically new approach to training animals, one that has had a lasting effect on all circus animal acts ever since.

Vladimir Durov's son, Vladimir, began his circus career in 1907 as a clown and satirist, working with trained animals. Unfortunately, he fell gravely ill and died in his prime in 1912.

Anatoly Durov's son, Anatoly, made his circus debut in 1914 in the city of Ryazan, but his real fame came in the years following the Revolution.

The Durov method became firmly established in the Soviet circus. In the first years after the Revolution the elder Vladimir Durov continued working in Durov's Corner, which he had established in 1909 and which is now a state scientific research laboratory. Durov first became interested in physiology in his youth, attending Professor I. M. Sechenov's lectures on higher nervous activity at Moscow University. It was only after the Revolution that he had an opportunity to devote himself to research in earnest. Durov evolved new methods of "painless training", based on the study of conditional reflexes in animals. All the best Soviet animal-trainers now follow this method. Durov is responsible for establishing a scientific basis for animal-training. The laboratory in which he conducted his experiments is now known as the Durov Museum and Animal

Theatre and is headed by Anna Durova, Vladimir Durov's daughter.

However, Vladimir Durov was not content to limit his activities to laboratory study. The call of the circus was too strong. Durov had given fifty years of his life to the circus and could not leave it now in his old age, not even for science.

Aided by the state, he renewed and greatly enlarged his animal troupe, returning to the circus arena in the early 20s. This was a new Durov. He had been a buffoon, a clown and a satirist, but now he was a clown and a lecturer, a clown and a scientist. This clown amused his audiences while teaching and explaining things to them. In his little opening speech he would say:

> *Now all my knowledge and my heart*
> *Are for the people.*

Then Durov would present his amazing animals, supplementing their performance with a running commentary on their behaviour in their natural surroundings, explaining how they had been taught to do the various tricks.

Vladimir Durov died in August 1934.

The younger Anatoly Durov performed with a large and varied group of animals, achieving fascinating results. At the same time, his commentary was always biting and topical. He, too, died an early death in 1928.

The Durov method in the Soviet circus as we know it today is associated with two men, Vladimir and Yuri Durov.

Vladimir Durov is the grandson of the elder Anatoly Durov and the nephew of the younger Anatoly Durov. He completed his education in Voronezh and then went on to study at the State Theatrical Studio of the Meyerhold Theatre.

Yuri Durov is another of Vladimir Durov's grandsons. After graduating from secondary school he became an apprentice in his grandfather's house, helping him out in Durov's Corner and appearing with him in his circus act.

There is much in common in the approach of the two Durov grandsons, and that is why their work is jointly reviewed here.

Both are talented animal-trainers who work with large and varied groups of animals. If we were to compare the troupes

Durov was the first Russian circus performer to treat comedy seriously, and this produced amazing results

His animals tried to act like humans

while he tried to see things from the animals' point of view,

to understand them

Grandpa Durov and his brother Anatoly were the founders of the Soviet school of the circus

of the elder Durovs with those of today, the present would certainly be the more interesting. At various times they have included performing elephants, seals, bears, hippopotamuses, camels, horses, foxes, cocks, a kangaroo, ostriches, dogs, pigs, parrots. monkeys and many other animals and birds. However, each animal has its own way of life, character and habits. Training methods which bring the desired results when working with a seal prove futile when working with an elephant. As a rule, animal-trainers prefer to work with a single species of animal. The very fact that the Durovs exhibit a large and varied group, achieving excellent results with the group as a whole, is further proof of their great experience and talent. One must never forget that the Durov animals do not perform out of fear (one actually feels like saying that they do so from a love of art). Undoubtedly, they are encouraged by their desire to receive a tasty morsel from the trainer's hand. The animals perform in a way that makes it seem as if they and the trainer are taking part in a merry game, one that gives pleasure to them all. The trainer must present an act that is well produced and perfectly cast. And the Durovs are talented producers and actors. Their performance is sincere, uninhibited, charming and graceful, and this despite their age and impressive weight. They create an image of warm-hearted, yet slightly ironic, kindly magicians who, at a touch of their wands, can transform ordinary animals into sensible creatures. Stories we have read in our childhood seem to materialise before our eyes in the circus arena. The traditional clowns' costumes the Durovs wear recall the magicians of yore: their kindly round faces are nearly devoid of make-up and their merry, mischievous eyes are in perfect harmony with the images they have created.

Perhaps other trainers do more complex tricks, but, as a whole, you will not find an animal act more entertaining and well-presented than the Durovs'. A seal juggles several balls and cones—in other words, it is performing its usual act. But when it has finished, it begins to clap a flipper against its stomach, demanding a fish as a reward for its performance. Having swallowed the fish, it begins to clap its flippers together furiously. And one feels that it is actually interested in the acclaim of the audience that it is demanding. The elephant has nine sticks with which it does various simple sums. But then someone gives it a problem in addition. The answer is clearly ten. What will the elephant do? It breaks the last stick in two and now has ten sticks instead of nine, thus solving the problem. There is no need to say how effective this trick is.

And what about the Durovs? They do not limit their participation to instructing their charges but take an active part in the proceedings supplying the commentary, and are in turn surprised, annoyed, ironic and happy. They are playing their parts, talking to the animals as if they were sensible creatures, becoming their partners in the act. Several skits are performed, some lyrical, some comical, but all have a beginning, a climax and an end. Each is presented to reveal some aspect of the animal's nature, there is always a dramatic conflict. Thus, a stubborn pony, sitting on the edge of the arena and prodded by the circus clowns, does not want to go back to the stables despite the trainer's coaxing and shouting. Suddenly, a well-behaved elephant wearing a patrolman's armband picks the pony's reins up in its trunk and drags it off. In another skit two cocks try to out-crow each other, each extremely jealous of its own performance.

Another member of the Durov clan, Anna Durova's granddaughter, Teresa Durova, has become famous in her own right and has developed a style of her own.

The Durovs have always been one of the main attractions of any circus performance, and their contribution to the art of the Russian and Soviet circus has been great, indeed. However, the challenge of the road ahead beckons, and that is something no Durov has ever been able to resist.

1963

IN THE CIRCUSES
OF EUROPE

By A. Gryaznov

"Vladimir Durov, who made his circus debut thirty years ago, belongs to a family of Russian animal-trainers already famous in the second half of the 19th century. Durov's uncle, Anatoly Durov, toured Belgium in the 20s. Some of you may still remember him."

Thus, in 1958, the Belgian press announced the coming tour of Vladimir Durov, People's Artiste of the R.S.F.S.R.

Durov was greeted warmly by his audiences. His animals appeared in all the newspapers and magazines, on TV and in the newsreels. According to the many hardened reporters covering the story, the "master trainer and his amazing caravanserai," were a sensation under the Big Top. Each and every act was magnificent: the elephant giving the juggling seal the correct time, the flying mice, the jumping foxes, the cocks and cats. In the finale Durov released hundreds of doves. His success was unprecedented: the audience rose as one man, the ovation was thunderous.

"Nothing is impossible as far as Durov is concerned. Not a single animal can hope to escape his thoughtful eye, and there is reason to believe that he will one day make goldfish jump through a hoop and flies march around on

Today the art of the animal-trainer has reached new heights: the elephant trained by the young Vladimir Durov introduces his master

The younger Durov's animals keep an eye on the clock. No overtime here

They are in step with the modern demands for accuracy

An elephant knows who his real friends are

In Durov's troupe everyone learns new tricks. Here a fox is practising high jumps

The bear is developing its will-power, but that bottle of milk is a sore temptation

This seal has a one-track nose

their hind legs!" This was how Durov was presented to Belgium's radio listeners.

News of the triumph of the Soviet circus was passed on by word of mouth. Crowds of Belgians and visitors to the Brussels World Fair stormed the administration offices and crowded round the Soviet performers. Thousands of people followed Durov on the street when he took his four-legged troupe for an airing during the small hours of the night. One could hear the applause blocks away when Baby the Hippo would suddenly stop in his walk to lick Durov's hand or the elephant would bow gracefully to the crowds.

The press described each of Durov's acts in detail. "Durov fires a pistol, but the dove sitting on the barrel doesn't even fly away. His fox and hen play happily together. There are a cat and rats who live in peace and friendship. Durov has turned all the old accepted maxims upside-down. He has pushed back the boundaries of what we consider to be reasonable and understandable. His choice of animals for his troupe is fantastic. Durov's hippopotamus even does somersaults."

Not many knew the unusual and nearly tragic story of Malysh ("Baby") the Hippo.

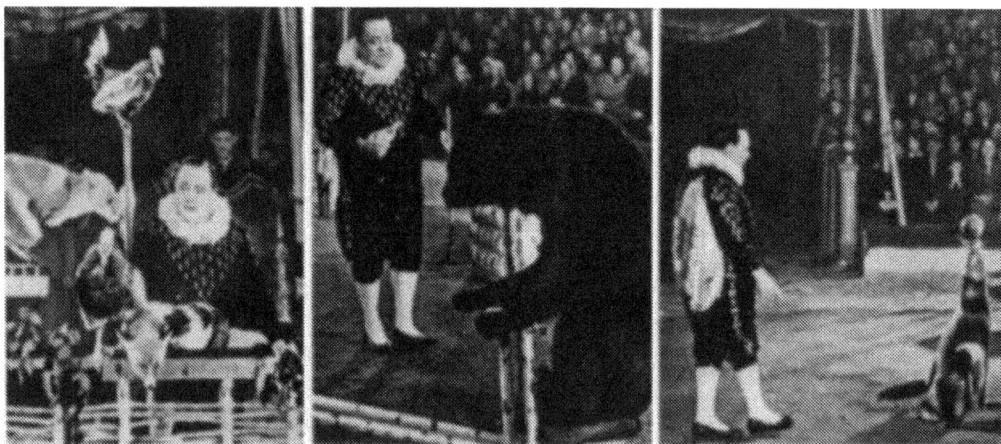

"It was the dream of my life," Vladimir Durov said. "As you know, all the men in our family were animal-trainers. My uncle, who died in 1928, bequeathed his troupe to me.

" 'You must love animals. They are completely within man's power,' my uncle said. 'Each and every one can be taught something. There is only one animal that cannot be trained. and that is a hippopotamus!' "

And here we have a hippopotamus in the circus arena.

"How long did it take you to train Baby?" a famous zoologist once asked Durov.

"A year," Durov said.

"Why, that's impossible! And what did you find most difficult?"

"Making the huge animal do somersaults."

Truly, the story of the performing hippopotamus is the story of the animal-trainer's feat. His success was based on the accumulated experience of the Russian and Soviet schools of animal training and on his own fundamental knowledge of nature and the animal world.

Vladimir Durov got Baby in 1956. He led the giant right into the ring and kept a close watch on him, to see what he liked. What were Baby's ways and habits? What was he capable of doing?

What wouldn't this kangaroo give for a second pair of gloves!

The leopard gets better with each successive performance

If this is supposed to be a dog's life ... well!

This is Baby. He and Durov are old friends. . .

*but size doesn't interfere with
a good performance*

Circus audiences will never forget Durov's favourite act. It stars his elephant, Masha Grey, and is called "The Gypsy Dance."

This is how it came into being.

During a rehearsal one of Durov's assistants climbed onto Masha's back. The animal was annoyed and tried to throw the man by shaking its shoulders. This first timid movement furnished the idea for the skit. Through repetition these movements gradually became established. Masha Grey was an instant success as a fiery gypsy dancer in many circuses of the world.

The elephant has been man's helper since ancient times. The hippopotamus has no such distant history. How then did Durov train Baby? This is what he says:

"As I watched Baby, I sensed in him a love for adventure. Of course, it was still too dangerous to take him out for walks, but he was always ready to explore the circus corridors and was even eager to climb the stairs to the upper floors. I put this inborn curiosity to use, encouraging it with kind words and tasty tidbits. Once, Baby fell head over heels and landed on his stomach. He was very frightened. But I calmed him with the magic word "Bravo," which all my animals know. Repeating this day after day and gradually increasing the range of his movements, I taught Baby to do somersaults in the ring."

The impossible had been achieved! Audiences took Baby to their hearts; they recognised him on his walks in the cities of the world.

We started out by saying that Baby's story was both unusual and nearly tragic. The tragic part occurred in Italy. The circus arena in Rome is slanted. Durov entered with Baby. He spoke to the hippo through a microphone. Baby became nervous. He was not used to the strange sound of a human voice coming over a microphone. The animal did not recognise it as the live, kind voice of its trainer. Baby did his act badly. The slanting floor made his tricks more difficult and he tired quickly. Durov recalls that he should have stopped the act at that point, that he was wrong in urging the animal on. Baby suddenly became angry, he lowered his head and made a dash for Durov. It took nerves of steel and great patience to calm the enraged hippo.

24

The flattering words of praise in newspaper reviews are a tribute to the trainer's courage and love for his chosen profession.

After watching one of the performances, Gianni Rodari, the well-known Italian author, wrote an article entitled "The Lunik of All Circuses Has Arrived from Moscow." "Vladimir Durov's Noah's ark is but one of the impossible acts which the Moscow Circus is presenting round the world and has now brought to Italy. His acts are a study in rhythm, high spirits and innovation."

Following is an excerpt from a review by Salvatore Quasimodo, "The Circus with an Ancient Past." "The inimitable Vladimir Durov trains animals according to a scientific method which excludes any form of pressure or force. This kindly trainer, convinced that coexistence is possible among peoples and, therefore, among animals, has brought together cocks and foxes and cats and mice and has taught hunted game to surrender to the victor to avoid unnecessary bloodshed." (He has in mind "The Hunter's Dream" in which no sooner does Durov shoulder his gun than ducks begin falling into his game bag.)

"The actor's skill, his friendliness towards his furred and feathered partners, be they wild beasts or domestic animals, are a guarantee of his popularity with any audience. Even when playing to reserved English audiences his act was invariably accompanied by laughter and applause."

There is reason why Durov receives hundreds of letters from fans, circus attendants, performers and actors in every country he has toured. Quite recently Robert Delnest, the well-known Belgian painter, sent Durov one of his monographs with the following inscription: "I am sending you this small work on Soviet art so you may know how I admire your great and wonderful country, its people and the creative spirit which is ever gaining momentum for the good of all mankind."

There were many words of praise and gratitude for the truly humane, artistic performances which Durov and his colleagues gave in France and Luxembourg. They were besieged by fans backstage and in the streets of Paris and Marseilles, Turin, Lyon, and Liège, for the language of the circus is indeed international. A gentleman came up to Durov after a press conference in Italy and confessed:

These two will never let each other down

"Señor Durov, I was really prejudiced against the Russians. I'll have to change my opinions now."

During an informal meeting of Soviet performers and the actors of the Unity Theatre in Great Britain there were songs in Russian and in English and many manifestations of friendship.

Durov's act is synonymous with performing animals. But these animals are not his captives. No member of the Durov dynasty has ever been seen brandishing a stick or a whip. The "actors" perform freely, mischievously and even with obvious pleasure. Herein lies not only the "secret" of their training, which is based on encouraging their natural instincts and habits, but of the humane nature of our art. The Soviet circus is known as "the arena of friendship," "the arena of peace."

1963

FALLOWIING
IN HIS
GRANDFATHER'S
FOOTSTEPS

By I. Guchek

The market square was full of ruts and puddles. To the left was the market and the fire-tower, to the right was a gloomy, barracks-type building, and straight ahead was a swamp, through which the one and only little road led to the Vspolye Railway Station. This is what Labour Square in the city of Yaroslavl looked like thirty years ago.

Here in the market-place, here in
*   the square,*
Stood the circus and tents of the fair,
Where Durov the Elder held forth from
*   the stage*
With gags that became all the rage.

Thus Yuri Durov, Merited Artiste of the R.S.F.S.R. and grandson of the great Vladimir Durov, began his performance in the beautiful new circus of Yaroslavl. The circus faces on a great square surrounded by tall new buildings and is crowded every night.

After the first intermission the m.c. announces the next act:

"Yuri Durov!"

Audiences greet him as an old friend, knowing they will not be disappointed. Then the animals go through their paces. The people are more amazed by their tricks than by the most daring acrobats. How can animals be made to do such things? This is the question most likely to be asked by fans backstage.

Yuri Durov is another member of the second generation of this famous circus family

When word was passed through the shops of the Yaroslavl Tire Factory that the circus had come and Yuri Durov was going to perform, the crowd that gathered in the main assembly hall would have gladdened the heart of any star. However, a factory lunch hour is not endless, and the conversation had to be continued after work hours in the factory club. This was for the best, since there were so many questions to be answered.

He always enters the ring like a prince

"I sometimes think that the public is more interested in how an animal-trainer achieves his results than in the performance of the animals themselves," Durov said. "In my forty years in the circus I have had innumerable talks with workers, collective farmers and soldiers. I performed for the autoworkers of Gorky, the cotton growers of Central Asia, the miners of Donbas, the wheat growers of the Ukraine, the workers of Magnitogorsk, Ivanovo and many other cities, on ships of the Merchant Marine and the Navy, for children in children's homes. And each and every performance has strengthened my belief that my choice of profession was correct, for it is loved and respected by the people.

"I began accompanying my grandfather on his numerous engagements at people's clubs, factories and plants when I was eight years old. Those were difficult times, we often found that there was not enough food for the animals, for this was during the Civil War in Russia. But there was so much optimism and joy in Vladimir Durov's performances! He realised that art, and the circus especially, must serve the people. 'I am the jester of His Majesty the People!' he would say proudly."

Durov picked up a tire-shaped ashtray, a gift from the workers of the Yaroslavl Tire Factory.

"My home museum is getting bigger," he said with a smile. "I have a miner's lamp from the miners of Donbas, a shotgun from the workers of Izhevsk, numerous photographs and other presents. I consider these my greatest reward, for they are constant reminders of my duty towards my people.

"I was in Yaroslavl at the outbreak of the war and spent the first few months there. It was a very difficult time, but we continued our performances and the public came to the circus. We toured factories, plants and military hospitals, and I saw that the war had not broken the people, that they were, as ever, interested in art."

Evening was approaching. The crowds were drawing towards the bright lights of the circular building on Labour Square, people were hurrying to spend an evening with Yuri Durov, the talented grandson of a famous grandfather who is furthering the wonderful traditions of the Durov circus dynasty.

1963

Every actor wants to know his audience

Anyone for the races today?

THE CLOWN,
COMEDY
AND TRAGEDY

By Viktor Shklovsky

The Volga Boatmen's Song was not always a mournful one. Originally, the leader would sing several stanzas, often rather coarse in content, and then would suddenly include the command of the refrain ("Pull, ye lads, pull!").

The stanzas were a momentary pause, a second's relaxation before straining every muscle. It was a method based on a deep knowledge of the laws of team-work.

The ancient religious feasts included scenes of hunting or tilling in which the people appealed to nature to be bountiful. This was accomplished by alternating the exalted and the base, for the ancient popular presentations were interspersed with wild merriment.

This was true also of the Australian corrobori —folk festivals. According to Y. Lips, a German naturalist, even the old men sitting in the "boxes" in the bushes would throw dignity to the winds and laugh till the tears streamed down their faces at the sight of the grotesque dances.

During the "Seal's Dance" of the feasts on Tierra del Fuego the jesters and clowns provided a break in the religious atmosphere. Among the primitive tribes of New Guinea the witch-doctors imitate "white men" and their modern devices. The people of Africa laugh at

Charlie Chaplin once said that his success was the success of a clown

Young and old, no one could resist his charm

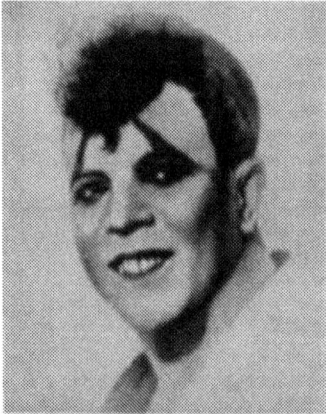

the ways of the Europeans and at their arrogant ignorance of life.

This combination of comedy and tragedy was preserved in the medieval passion plays and in the plays of Shakespeare, providing further proof that they were based not only on religious tradition but on a knowledge of the laws of art.

The lama's gods wore magnificent masks in the religious dances of ancient Tibet. Suddenly, jesters would break into the proceedings, copying in a grotesque manner the solemn walk of the sacred masks, evoking laughter from the audience.

The Greek tragedies were relieved by the merriment of the satyrs. Comedy and tragedy were divided according to theme and were written independently of each other, but both were based on the same mythological subject-matter and both were presented during the same festivities. This combination of comedy and tragedy heightened the perception.

The jester and the clown still rule the circus ring today. There is no tragedy to supplement comedy here, but there is an ever-present feeling of fear.

We fear for the lives of the aerialists, whose courage far surpasses our own, we watch the animal-trainers and wild beasts, the daring

Vitaly Lazarenko

Karandash, like Chaplin, is a tender clown

Konstantin Berman is a melancholy clown who thinks that nothing is as funny as his fellow humans

bareback riders, the tightrope-walkers. All these pent-up emotions are relieved by the clown's cavorting.

The clown has held his audiences in attention for thousands of years. He is the distant echo of tragedy. Shakespeare has proven the immortality of tragedy presented in an every-day manner. King Lear's friend is the Fool; the gravedigger who speaks to Hamlet is also a jester, though he does not wear the robes of the clown.

According to ancient Russian tradition, a jester accompanied the wedding party. He was entwined with green-pea vines, the traditional "Green-pea Jester," the symbol of fertility.

The clown and jester are not simply the ones who get slapped. A jester may be touching. Pierrot, Harlequin and the beautiful Colombine used different means to express the same emotions.

Molière has preserved the traditional jester in high comedy, but there is no need to think that we must part with the merry clown. Mayakovsky's *Mystery-Buff* is an echo of the medieval passion play, though its concept of Heaven and Hell is quite different, and it has many contemporary circus jests. The theatre has never found it possible to discard the clown either.

While Boris Vyatkin is a member of the jolly clique

Yuri Nikulin, the phlegmatic one wishes someone would make him laugh

Oleg Popov, the "Sunny Clown", made his circus debut in 1951, and no one has been more happy than his audiences

Igor Ilyinsky, one of the outstanding Soviet comedians, made his debut in the Meyerhold Theatre, playing the part of the Failure in *The Great Cuckold*. Ilyinsky's name has become a byword in the Soviet cinema, but his talent has never been fully tapped, although in recent times he has created several delightful grotesque and realistic types. Given the right scenario, Ilyinsky would certainly join Chaplin's ranks.

In *Limelight* Chaplin revived the traditions of the Commedia dell' Arte. The old clown is Pierrot, the composer is Harlequin, while Colombine has hardly been changed at all and even performs a little dance at the end of the tragedy.

The Soviet circus is now in its prime. Each time I attend a circus performance I find that the circus has reached new heights.

This is the spring of the Soviet circus, and the Soviet clown has also blossomed forth. Oleg Popov has amazed the world, he has even astounded Charlie Chaplin, though it is difficult to amaze an actor in his own field. A clown's success is always hard-earned, for his is the success of laughter, and it is by far more difficult to make people laugh than to make them cry. A circus audience is straightforward and unconvinced. Thus, Oleg Popov's success is one of the principle. This clown is not drenched in flour, he is an ordinary man, he is not humiliated. Popov's commentary is new and touching. During a performance in Paris he walked down a slack wire to where Josephine Baker sat in the audience and placed a big red cloth heart at her feet. And Paris applauded, because Paris itself had laid its heart at the feet of the great actress and singer.

A performance by Yuri Nikulin brought to mind *People Alone by Themselves*, by Maxim Gorky, written in 1923.

There is a scene in which Gorky describes an English clown bowing to himself respectfully. As Gorky recalls it, the clown stood before a mirror, "removed his top hat and bowed respectfully to his image".

Man alone by himself is sad, sometimes touchingly helpless and, therefore, comical. Further in the story we read: "I saw Anton Chekhov in his garden, trying to catch a sunbeam with his hat and, quite unsuccessfully, to put both on his head. And I saw that his failure annoyed the sunbeam-catcher, his face became angrier and angrier."

"Lev Tolstoi asked a lizard softly:

" 'Are you happy?'

"It was sunning itself on a rock in some bushes along the road and he stood in front of it, his fingers stuck in his belt. Then, looking round cautiously, the great man confessed to the lizard:

" 'I'm not.' "

In this collection there are observations of women, clowns, great writers and scientists. And it becomes apparent that all of them, when alone, are unusual, that all reveal something of their inner nature.

I think that in recent times the collective spirit of the country has matured the Soviet clown. He has wiped the ricepowder from his face, the rouge from his nose, he has taken off his oversize shoes and has become younger, more attractive, more graceful. He plays the part of an ordinary man who seems to have forgotten for several long moments that people are watching him, and he lives for himself, he is a simple, touching person.

A miracle has taken place in the Soviet circus ring, it is as if we have glimpsed an ordinary person under a magnifying glass in the spotlight. No, this is no small person. He is no longer the perpetual failure created by Chaplin. This is a full-fledged human being. He is comical in quite a different way and no longer appears to be helpless. He is funny in the inexperience of youth, in the fact that he has discarded the conventions of life without discarding his humaneness. A miracle is being born in the circus ring that can serve the Soviet theatre and the Soviet cinema as well. There is a reason why the great Chaplin followed Oleg Popov about Paris as a man follows a torch-bearer down dark streets.

The man in the ring has become brighter and the laughter he evokes is brighter, too.

1962

MY HERO

By Oleg Popov

I was born in 1930. This was a time of great change, a time of building socialism in our country. The new way of life was taking a firm stand. When I was a little boy I spent hours watching blocks of new houses going up, replacing the crooked lanes and dilapidated structures of our quiet section on the outskirts of Moscow. New factories were built, and from our house we could hear the rumbling, heavily-laden freight trains.

I think that had I lived in other times I would not have had such a clear understanding of the role of the common man in the affairs of his country, of the great power of labour and the might of the working man's hands.

When I was a schoolboy people who had but recently been employed in small domestic industries became workers in the largest factories. We boys looked upon them with awe. And we dreamed about our future. Life itself supplied the fuel for our dreams. We wanted to be pilots, drivers of the first Soviet automobiles. sailors, locomotive drivers and even ticket collectors at the new Dynamo Stadium. But we were still at school and our dreams were still a far way off. Often on a hot summer's day we were summoned by the familiar sound of

I decided to become a clown because there are still too many problems in the world

Nothing like a little rest after a hard day's work

I always say men are the best cooks

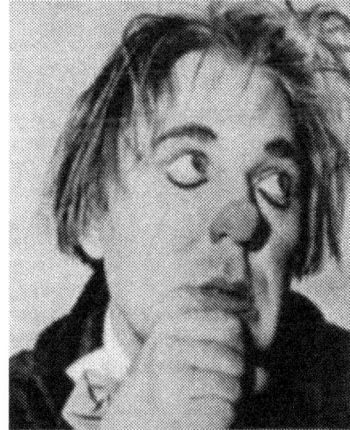

an organ-grinder, and a bored parrot would pull out slips of paper with our fortunes printed on them.

I went to the circus several times when I was a boy and always associated its noise and splendour with a really festive occasion. I sat there with bated breath, absorbing each movement, fearful lest I miss the main event. I liked the animal-trainers, I was fascinated by the skill of the jugglers, the acrobats and tightrope-walkers, but I always derived the greatest pleasure from the clown, a red-headed man who made everyone laugh. Sometimes there were two clowns: Bim-Bom or Pat and Pataschon. When I came home I tried to imitate them. I tried training the neighbourhood cats and dogs for my act, but they would flee at the very sight of me the next day. And everyone would laugh.

In 1943, I became a fitter's apprentice at the Pravda Printing Works. After working hours I went in for sports and especially took to acrobatics. Soon I was a nember of the Krylya Sovetov Sports Club. There were many youths my age there and several among them had their hearts set on becoming circus acrobats. I watched them perform with envy, and soon we became friends. We learned to do various tricks.

Just give a man a good car

One evening my new friends took me to a small building on a quiet street near the Pravda plant. The plaque outside read: State Circus School. I was still quite young and understood the words literally to mean: here is the step which will take ordinary boys to the heights of circus skill. How could I pass it by?

I became an unfrequent and, later, a regular visitor and finally got to know some of the students there. I was drawn irresistibly to the gymnasts and the acrobats and tried to copy what they did right there with them in the school gym. They in turn helped me all they

could. Thus, little by little, I made my way in the circus school, until one really fine day I became a full-fledged student. Under the watchful eye of Alexander Sosin, the oldest circus instructor who was in charge of the children's group, I gradually mastered the skills of the circus performer.

One summer, when my friends and I were in the country, we stretched a wire between two trees. I climbed up jokingly and tumbled right

They say a happy marriage is one where interests are shared. I didn't want to take any chances and so talked my wife into clowning, too

off. Everyone had a good laugh, but I became angry and wondered what had gone wrong and why I was worse than the others.

From that day on I began to sneak away into the forest where I would string the cursed wire between two trees, climb up, fall off, climb up again, and fall off again, and so on until I was exhausted. And I never noticed how I eventually learned to stand on the wire, keep my balance and move along it. This brought a true feeling of satisfaction.

When I came back to school that autumn I showed off my new accomplishment. Sergei Morozov, my teacher and instructor, quite unexpectedly suggested that I rehearse an act under his direction. It was to be called "Balancing on a Slack Wire". I was both happy and shy as I accepted the offer.

And so the endless rehearsals began. After rehearsals we would discuss ways of making the act more interesting. Many hours were spent in thinking up new tricks, in trying them out and perfecting them. One of the tricks I thought of then has remained in my act till this day: while standing on the slack wire I sneeze. This makes my cap fly off. It lands on the tip of the cane I have behind my back, and I begin a long and futile search for it, turning and twisting in all directions.

Sergei Morozov taught me everything I know about rope-walking. He spent much time with me, offering valuable suggestions, teaching me the various tricks of the trade. In return, he demanded persistence and put me through endless rehearsals.

I made my debut in 1949. On a hot July day a nineteen-year-old boy entered the circus arena and portrayed a man who had unexpectedly found himself on a tightwire. Though the man was terribly afraid of falling, he had the courage to juggle balls and a cane, swaying and

My daughter taught me this routine

careening in the most hazardous way. And then, at the most difficult moment, I heard the sound of laughter and applause, the first applause in my life. And right then and there, standing on the tightwire, I realised that I had passed the test and was now a real circus performer.

However, something I heard during the performance that day made me later stop and take stock of myself. A man in the audience said:

"Young man, you're not a rope-walker, you're a clown!"

Me, a clown? Somehow, it didn't sound right. In my mind's eye I saw the clown's traditional painted face, red nose, shiny bald head or bushy wig. No, I could never be like that and never wanted to be like that. Why, then, had he said I was a clown? Perhaps the secret of a clown's success lay not in his appearance but in something else, in something deeper. What could it be?

And my search began. It was a search into everyday life, into everything. The work I did after graduating from the circus school was a continuation of this search for an image of a clown that would be my own. I now worked in a regular circus, where my new colleagues helped me, as my teachers continued to do. However, the greatest aid I received was from persons who did not even know the part they were

Here you see me as a mighty rajah,

and a mighty chicken tender,

and a mighty fine fellow, too

playing in my life. These were the best clowns of our times, the popular circus favourites. As I watched them, studied their technique, searched out the secrets of their skill, I discovered a new significance in the clown's cavorting.

* * *

A performance has begun. The audience watches the amazing acrobats and gymnasts, the magician's tricks, the jugglers and the wild animals. Various types of acts make up a circus programme. Is this merely a haphazard collection, or is there something that binds these acts together, something that erases the short pauses between them, filling in the minutes and preparing the audience for the next thrill? Yes, there is such an art, a special type of art which is the cement that joins the separate parts into a single performance. This is the art of the circus clown.

He runs or trots out into the limelight, naïvely determined to repeat that which both he and the audience have just admired so greatly in the previous act. He is clumsy and stumbles, he falls and gets into all sorts of tangles but in the end he finally manages to repeat in a comical and skilled way everything the others have done. The audience laughs, they are pleased.

And then it is time for the next act to go on.

There is much sadness in the world. So I became a doctor, to cure people of their melancholy

True, you don't know what sort of a patient you'll get next

But all's well that ends well

There is something so very familiar about the clown. We recognise our own shortcomings, the clown's satire is gentle, yet biting at times, but it is always funny. At the same time, it blends unobtrusively with the acts on the programme that present the best of human qualities: skill, courage and beauty.

The circus is ablaze with light. An act has just gone off, the applause is dying down. Then a funny figure appears in the empty ring. We see

I use group therapy on children

a small man being led out by a small donkey. The donkey looks strange. It has bicycle handlebars hanging on its neck, a seat on its back and a licence plate dangling from its rump. The little man takes down a pump and begins to "inflate" the donkey's hind leg. Then he mounts his live bicycle and rides around the ring.

In the next pause between acts the little man is pushed into a tank of seals. He climbs out and dries off by pinning himself to a clothesline with a big clothespin.

Now we see him in the ring again. This time he has a shaggy little dog with him. The dog barks long and loud into a microphone. Then the man removes his hat and announces:

"You have just been listening to a speech by Herr Goebbels, Minister of Propaganda."

Who is the actor? He has appeared in many guises, but in each and every one he has made the audience laugh and applaud. His name is Karandash, and he is one of the most popular Soviet circus clowns.

In the autumn of 1927, Moscow's Circus School opened its doors to its first pupils. This was the first real circus school in the world. It enrolled future jugglers and acrobats, clowns and comedians. One of the three hundred hopefuls who applied was Mikhail Rumyantsev, the future Karandash.

Those were difficult times. The new was being born by breaking the old traditions. What should a circus clown be like? This was a question which as yet had no clear answer. The clowns in the various Russian circuses were appearing as Pat and Pataschon, Charlie Chaplin or just plain buffoons. Though these were all tried and true visages, the very fact of their being traditional was meeting with an ever greater protest on the part of the circus youth and audiences.

In the more difficult cases I have to use my musical toothbrush

Mikhail Rumyantsev, the son of a Petersburg fitter and circus clown, was one of the innovators.

He graduated from the Circus School in 1930 and began appearing in the guise of Charlie Chaplin. However, in presenting "the little man from the big city" Rumyantsev changed the social content of the image. He was never one to copy the style or mannerisms of other circus clowns. He was attuned to his surroundings and to life itself and this gradually changed his style: the melancholy failure, the "sad" clown, was transformed into a happy-go-lucky, humorous fellow.

During a performance for the workers of a tractor plant Rumyantsev felt more keenly than ever that it was time for him to discard his Chaplin guise, for it was dead in the face of the new way of life that was opening up before the people. Thus, the changeover began.

In 1936, a little man entered the arena of the Leningrad Circus. He wore a baggy black coat, a striped shirt with a long string tie and unusually baggy black trousers. A look under his comical hat revealed an open, smiling face, both lively and wholesome, with just a trace of mischief and cunning and at times a comical seriousness which one so often finds in children.

Patients should never be afraid of their doctor

Our long talks always end on a happy note

It was the famous Karandash. In the course of three years he had won the hearts of his audiences by his vivid, yet simple performances. Karandash was assisted by his lovable partners, his little black donkey and his two Scotch terriers, Pushok and Toby.

Once, when Karandash was talking to us, a group of students, he said:

"So you want to know the difference between a Russian clown and a clown in the West? Well, Durov said that a Russian clown is witty, while a German clown tries to take funny tumbles and his wit is mostly limited to his feet. I never forgot these words and have always tried to put meaning into my act.

"My clown is curious and thus often finds himself in a comical predicament. My clown is a normal, healthy, smiling man, very active, always on the go, one who reacts with childish naïveté to every funny situation. He has his nose in everything, and he is not alone, he is one with the audience, with the masses. There is something both confident and wholesome about him, it is the optimism that is an integral part of every Soviet person."

"Why have you chosen this costume?" we asked.

"It evolved gradually. But I can tell you now that it has been a successful choice."

Rumyantsev showed us what he meant. He could bend and twist the soft felt hat into any shape, making it now a dunce cap, now a porkpie, depending upon his mood. His baggy pants made it easy for him to portray a woman crossing a puddle; besides, they were an excellent hiding-place for a mouse, a cat, or a hedgehog. And then there was his black suit. Black ennobles the circus clown, it gives him the right to join any audience, it makes it easier for him to establish contact with his audience.

One day, an hour before I was to go on, I decided that I couldn't clown through my whole life and wrote a sketch about a little man,

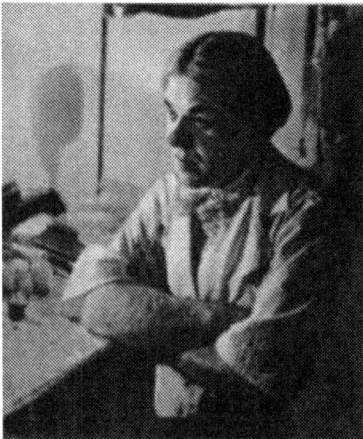

Karandash's clowning is wholesome and truthful. He was the first to appear as a positive comical character in the circus, one full of agility, skill and wit; Karandash became a satirist-clown. He was the first to blaze a new path, to deviate from the crude, traditional style of clowning.

I once spoke to the famous circus clown Boris Vyatkin in his dressing-room. We were surrounded by various props: a giant spoon, papier-mâché weights and Neptune's trident. The walls were covered with photographs. Here one could follow Vyatkin's career, from circus acrobat to clown. There was a picture of him as a young acrobat, photos which portrayed him when he was a gymnast, a clowning musician and a juggler, and in every one he appeared full of fun and wit. It seemed that no one could understand a clown's work better than he.

One morning in the city of Komsomolsk-on-Amur a new clown made his appearance. Many recognised the acrobat they had known before, but this time he was dressed in a red wig and wore huge shoes.

Vyatkin first appeared in the Moscow Circus in 1942. Soon he and a group of other performers were off to perform for the soldiers at the front. Boris Vyatkin put on more than 1,500 shows for the troops during the war. *who was looking for his place under the sun*

in order to drink a bottle of milk in peace

Thus, contemporary themes took their place in my act. I even had a synthetic cow

Many former soldiers remember the jolly clown who invariably appeared on a makeshift stage with a tiny twig for "camouflage."

Vyatkin returned to the circus in 1945. But this was no longer the traditional buffoon. Here was a clown without a wig, dressed in a green hat and an ordinary coat. He was a lively jester, a quick-witted fellow like many another jolly wit. But he could be serious if need be. The audience greeted him like an old friend. Where had they met before? Ah, yes, at the office. Or was it in the street? Or perhaps at a friend's house?

Cheerfulness and ease are qualities that are hard to come by for an actor. They are the result of concerted effort and long searching. Vyatkin has always strived to perfect his technique.

Boris Vyatkin is especially wonderful in his parodies of other circus acts. He mimicks the lion-tamers and strong men and makes fun of the old-fashioned clichés that are still a part of some acts. In the twinkling of an eye he is transformed into an empty-headed girl and chatterbox.

Vyatkin gradually went on to talking bits. His success was the result of hard work on the part of the jolly fellow in the red coat and green hat accompanied by his dog Manyunya, truly a canny, lively fellow from a big city.

We shall leave Boris Vyatkin now to say a few words about his "opposite," Alexei Shliskevich of the Riga Circus.

Here is a well-built, broad-shouldered man. He has a kindly face and somewhat naïve eyes. He is dressed in a regular suit with a long tie,

and an honest-to-goodness personal rocket ship

I know all about the Olympics, and I'm not giving up hope

flat-footed shoes and a checkered cap. This is Shliskevich in the ring.

Let's have a closer look. We see a very charming and friendly man with man's usual shortcomings. He's not a foolish fellow, trusting and hard-working, yet he is clumsy in everything he does. Shliskevich's long, dangling arms are extremely expressive. He knows how to use them unerringly in presenting a whole gallery of types to his audience. We see him as a house painter, a tailor, a barber and a janitor. And in each of his impersonations there is the spark of folk humour and optimism. The audience never roars, it smiles good-naturedly. This is the kindly smile with which we greet an old friend, this is Shliskevich's goal. "It's always better to underplay than to overplay," is a phrase he likes to repeat. In this, his motto, we find his style of playing a part with gentle, cautious humour. This sense of tact and moderation raise his performance to a high level, helping him to create many different character types.

I had yet another teacher, Konstantin Berman, the circus clown. He was a mischievous young fellow with a large, bulbous nose. He had a black moustache and sharp darting eyes, the eyes of a curious, sociable man who liked

I like my act to have sparkle

And if I while away my time by the fire, it's only when I'm working

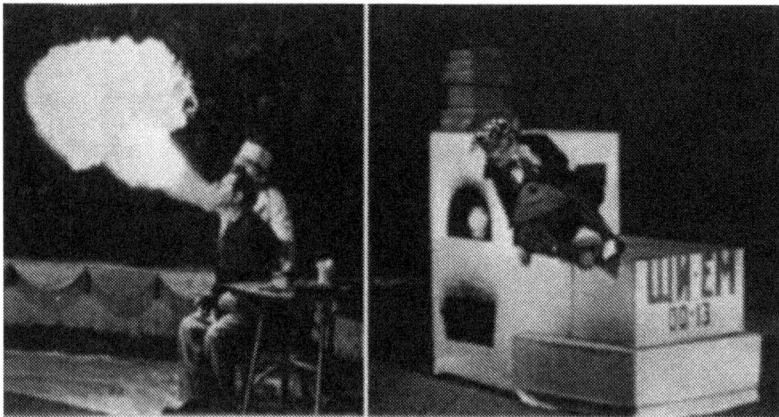

to poke his nose into other people's affairs. True enough, a moment after Berman appeared in the ring he was busy taking part (helping and getting in the way) in other acts, but either helping too vigorously or else suddenly becoming bored with it all. He was dressed in a white tuxedo that both emphasised and parodied the current demands of "good taste."

Berman is a universal performer. He is a juggler and an acrobat, a tightrope-walker and magician. He perfected these various skills in his childhood and youth, when he and his brother began their careers as circus clowns. At the beginning, his popularity lay in the fact that he could take any circus role. He used his skills to parody magnificently the previous acts on the bill.

Thus, the pantomimist-clown was born. He toured the Soviet Union and many foreign countries, and everywhere he performed he was well received, for audiences understand the vivid and expressive language of pantomime.

His success was a challenge to go onward, and onward meant to be a part of life, to express it in a witty joke, a satire, a happy word. And then Konstantin Berman uttered his first words in the ring. It was not easy in the beginning, for he had to overcome a slight speech defect. However, in a clown's difficult life this was the least of his worries.

The new clown and satirist made his appearance in the ring in 1946. He was excellent at witty banter on current events and knew how to present a bit of interesting news from a clown's mischievous point of view. One of his acts took him around the world on the *Rocket*. His ship called in many ports and in each the audience was treated to a number of funny incidents. In another skit Berman was put in charge of a group of clowns. Then he became the manager of a circus, then the manager of all the circuses. And he began to grow. He grew bigger and bigger and soon could not recognise any of his old friends or employees, until, finally, he got so huge that he burst.

These were all wonderful skits. Now, thinking back to the time, I am proud that I was on the same programme with Konstantin Berman at the Moscow Circus. He was much more than a partner and colleague. Before and after our performances Berman would spend hours teaching me, correcting my mistakes, giving me valuable suggestions, never trying to overshadow the beginner but always setting me in front of himself, making way for me.

One of the characteristics of the Soviet circus is its multi-national nature. Performers of the various national circuses create their acts on the basis of their own national traditions. The ring is brightly lit again and I anxiously await the entrance of the clown.

The strains of oriental music fill the arena as Hodja Nasreddin rides into the ring on a little donkey. He is dressed in a colourful robe. Yes, it really is Hodja Nasreddin, the hero of Eastern folklore, the kind-hearted simpleton. Though he seems rather dim-witted, we sense that he is truly clever and resourceful, that he has a wonderful sense of humour and a wealth of common sense. Today's Nasreddin is Akram Yusupov. Merited Artiste of the Uzbek Republic, a great master of the ring. His witty sayings supplement his skill in performing in the various circus genres.

While sitting astride his donkey, he calls out his greeting to the rope-walkers. There then ensues a comic tightrope scene that is close to my heart. Yusupov is sent back and forth from one end to the other several times. He keeps rushing back and forth with a comic look of consternation on his face, impersonating a victim of "bureaucracy."

Akram Yusupov's talent is evident in the convincing manner of his acting and miming. He uses these seemingly simple means to establish contact with his audiences, who are full of sympathy and understanding for the lively, realistic Hodja the clown has created.

I was very impressed by the following excerpt in L. Tanti's book, *The Soviet Circus:* "The old style of clowning, with its techniques and principles of building an act, and the ever-present 'buffoon' is dying away, mostly because the audience wants to see a lively, natural man. The appearance of degenerates, paralytics, idiots, maniacs and other forms of the insane (and this is the psycho-physical basis of all 'buffoon' types) can no longer hold the interest of the Soviet audience. Indeed, how many such 'clowns' unchanging in their traditions and traditional in their unchanging nature resemble a living person? It is impossible to compare them with any human being even though we make the necessary allowances for exaggeration, parody and jest. But all clowns must be people: they are connivers, muddleheads, scoundrels, merrymakers, bullies, sleepy-heads and braggarts, but they are living, breathing people, bits of actual reality."

As I read these words I saw in my mind's eye Karandash, Boris Vyatkin, Shliskevich, Berman and Yusupov, all of whom are united by a realistic approach in which one image complements and is a continuation of another. It was then that I, a pupil of Karandash, Berman and a host of other wonderful pranksters, decided that in the future I would also appear in a realistic guise that would not in itself be a cause for laughter.

Once, when I was appearing in Saratov in my tightrope skit, Borovikov, the clown that filled in all the breaks between the acts, fell ill. The manager knew that I dreamed of becoming a clown and that I had been practising by myself, and so he suggested that I fill in for Borovikov, who also asked me to go on. Borovikov said he was sure I'd make out all right. As I did not have a clown's costume, he lent me his own.

And so one evening I came into the ring dressed in another man's clothes and appearing in a new guise. It certainly was a case of stage fright, but I was met with applause and the sound of it followed me out as well. For the next twenty days I fought my timidity and constraint and went on as a clown every night, each time feeling more and more confident of myself.

Then the tour was over. My next engagement was in Riga, but I arrived there as a clown, not a rope-walker.

I gratefully returned Borovikov's costume and was now faced with the dilemma of what to wear. It had to be something original, something that was mine alone. I went through dozens of costumes, hats and caps, trying out their effect on me and on the audience, and then discarded them, one and all. Once, while rummaging in the circus dressing-room, I came upon a large checkered cap. A. Sudakevich, the circus artist, suggested I wear a black suit with it and blouse in the style of a Russian zipun. She sketched the outfit on a sheet of paper. A black suit! It immediately brought to mind Karandash and seemed truly to be a symbol of future success.

I decided I would be a plain Russian lad, Ivan the Fool of fairy-tale fame, who, in the end, is no fool at all. At the same time, I would be an average man of today with a good dose of simplicity, cunning, mischief and joy thrown in. The image would be a modern one, understandable to the working man. I would be aided by straw-coloured hair, a baggy blouse and a shy and clumsy manner. I know that such an appearance would be closer to the audience than any other. It is a composite image, and to achieve it means to discover the key to success. I wanted to be like Berman and Karandash, and what I had created was both like and unlike them.

Many of my young friends took an active part in writing my material. Success did not come at once, the road to it lay through mistakes and failure, but hard work conquered all.

Now the first stage had been completed, the time of searching and discovery was over. I entered upon the second stage of my career, that of perfecting my knowledge and skills.

In my mind this stage is connected with such Soviet cities as Riga, Voronezh, Kemerovo, Novosibirsk, Khabarovsk, Vladivostok and many others. Everywhere I went I discovered something new that I could put to use. Each of the cities I played in are not merely remembered as stops on the way, but as stages of my growth. It is wrong to think that I travelled a smooth road to success, it was in fact a bumpy, unpaved road full of ruts and pitfalls. My travels along it were difficult, but fascinating. Each step brought its own problems, it was impossible to go on before each problem had been tackled and solved. At this time my task was not to find my own stage identity, but to collect material for my act. The two qualities that ensured its popularity were its biting and topical nature. I wanted to reflect everything I saw in life, to unmask the grafters and bureaucrats and to rejoice at the success of our great plans.

The audiences themselves were a great help. At our public conferences they voiced their suggestions, they sent in letters with descriptions of new tricks and comical situations. The writers who created new skits were also of great help. But there was much I myself had to ponder over, for I alone knew what I could do and what experience I had to draw on. The years during which I had worked as a fitter came in very handy, for I often made my own props. This familiarity with the props was a definite advantage in the ring.

56

The days flew by in an endless series of rehearsals, in working with producers, script writers and my partners. Never once did I forget that the audience was the chief judge of my work and that no matter how complex a trick might be, I must always remain the same simple, familiar and jolly clown. I knew that the right image and the right attitude were the key to any circus performer's success. I had come to this realisation while touring the Soviet Union when my realistic clown was invariably well received by audiences. This truth was driven further home when I performed at the International Circus Festival in Warsaw and later at the Sixth Youth and Student Festival in Moscow. It became crystal-clear during our European tour.

This is what a French columnist wrote of me as a clown: "Popov does not appear in the ring dressed in a spangled suit with a dunce's cap, with a floured face and a rubber nose. He appears wearing a huge cap, of the kind Russian children wear in plays by Russian writers. His trousers are too short and he has on outsize girl's shoes, but nothing seems out of place. His hair is long and as straight as a stick. His large naïve blue eyes are never accentuated by make-up. His appearance causes no sensation. In fact, he seems to come stealthily into the ring, no burst of laughter greets him, there is no excited whispering, of the kind that greeted Fratellini in his exquisite costume. Popov comes out on tiptoe. He begins at zero and establishes a strong bond with his audience."

While touring France, Belgium, and England I observed the famed clowns of the West very carefully. The distinguishing feature of their work is an absence of any social content. The clowns of the West, from the famous Fratellini down to the young beginner, have isolated themselves from the pressing, day-to-day social and political problems that are uppermost in the minds of the people, they are wholly dependent upon their managers and must reconcile themselves to their role of pranksters and jesters. There was such face-slapping during these acts that I sometimes had the feeling there was more slapping than applause.

As I observed the circuses of capitalist countries I came to understand more clearly the distinguishing feature of our Soviet school of clowning, one that has social content and definite artistic aims. The red-headed clown cannot see the

Karandash was my teacher. His shadow follows me everywhere

world from behind his grotesque mask, the one and only image he has created for all times. But a comedian is much closer to reality, he is a real, live person, close to the heart of every working man.

* * *

Thinking of the future makes one dream. In our time, as Soviet culture blossoms, one cannot help thinking of creative growth and perfection. It is difficult to speak of what can be accomplished or of what has already been accomplished. Before the audience has sat in judgement of your work you can never be sure of success. But there are many things I want to do. I want to add new satirical, topical and comic skits to my act. I want to further develop my stage personality, to push back the accepted boundaries and bring in new methods, ones that are close both to the circus and the variety show.

In October 1960, I joined a group of Soviet circus performers for a tour of France where I had been four years before. Representing the art of the Soviet circus abroad was not only a great honour for us but a serious test as well.

As I listened to the applause in the circuses of Paris, Lyons and Marseilles I could not help recalling the past. This past was the circus school that made me an actor, the school that is now training new performers from among talented Soviet boys and girls.

Each year a new group of jugglers, rope-walkers and, naturally, clowns, leaves the Circus School. The clowns of my own generation, Nikulin and Shuidin, Mozel and Savich, keep on perfecting their art. Coming up behind them are the youngest generation of clowns, Kolobov, Nikolayev, Yanovskis and Yengibarov.

I belong to their ranks. My greatest wish is that all my comrades understand the great importance of creative searching and plain hard work.

1961

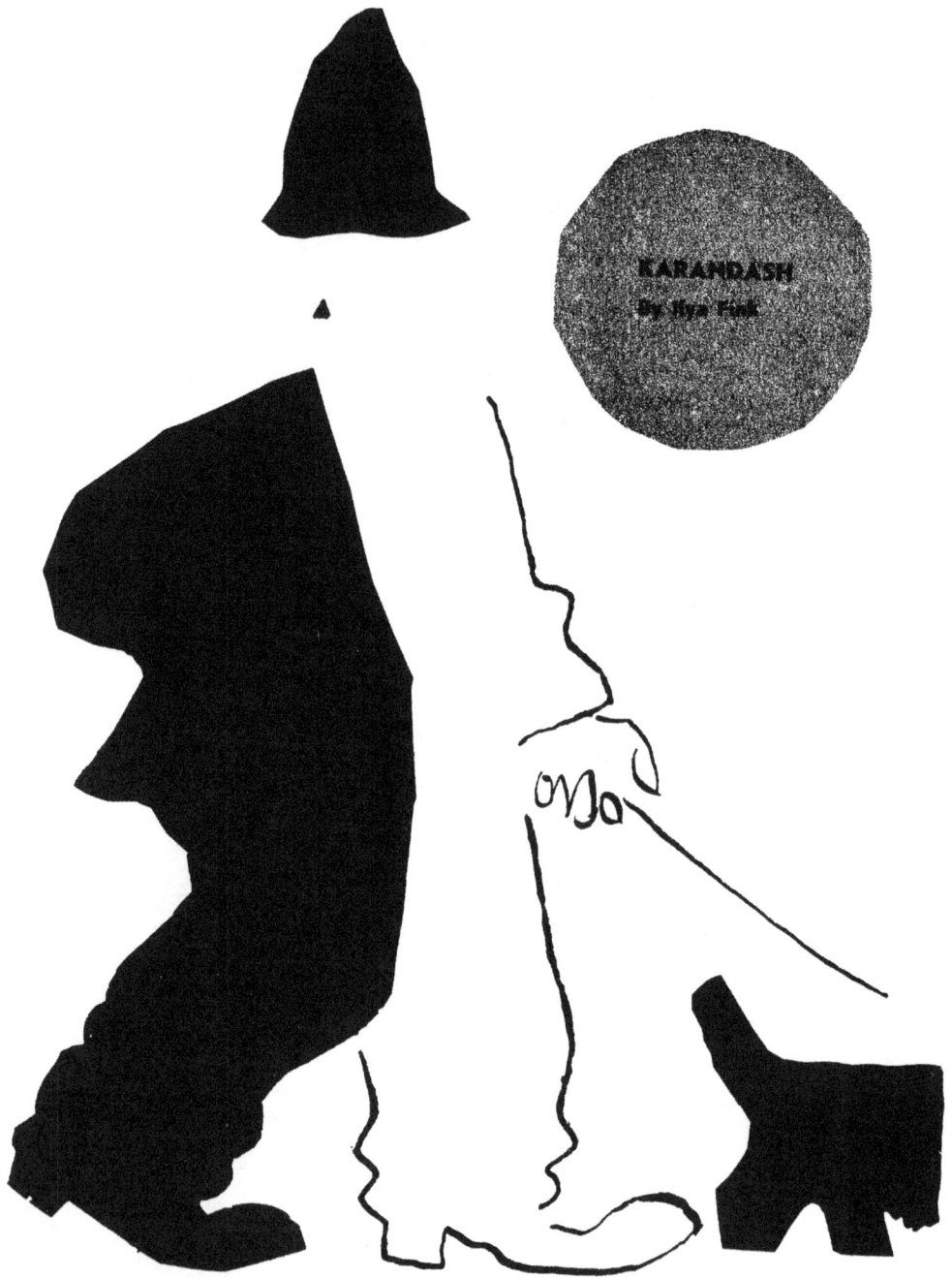

KARANDASH
By Ilya Fisk

A circus performance was on. When the lively overture ended the performers took their traditional bows and were gone. Now there was a feeling of expectation and excitement in the air, a feeling beloved since childhood.

Suddenly, a small, mischievous figure appeared in the brightly-lit ring. It was Karandash!

He always appears at the exact moment he is awaited, when the audience is at attention, when the unspoken question "Where is Karandash?" hangs suspended in the air.

He has hardly ever misjudged his timing. It is the sixth sense of an actor who is used to meeting his audiences alone.

In the Soviet circus we have long since come to know the actor-clown who puts on merry skits that often transcend in meaning a simple "filling-in" of the time between acts.

The art of the clown has become traditional. Today few people look back to the long, steep road along which this complex art developed, an art that was actually reborn in the Soviet circus.

The circus clown is usually presented as a stupid failure, a fool, as one who is invariably slapped in the face.

Here he is in person—Karandash!

He's one of Chaplin's followers. As you see, he also has a baggy suit and outsized shoes. Life itself provides the source of all his fun

Once, when he was out walking in the park, he accidentally knocked over a statue

And now there has appeared a new type of clown, a resourceful, clever merrymaker who has created a believable artistic image, a master of the witty, satirical skit.

Such was the road traversed. One of the first to blaze the way was Mikhail Rumyantsev, better known as Karandash.

In the autumn of 1927, a shy twenty-year-old youth from the town of Staritsa arrived in Moscow. Twice he took the entrance examinations at the newly founded Circus School and twice he failed. No special talents, very small in stature and rather frail was the verdict of his examiners.

But the youth was accepted on probation.

By a stroke of good luck the unfortunate lad was taken on as a clown with a group of circus students leaving on a practice tour of the provinces.

This tour determined his future.

Rumyantsev threw himself wholeheartedly into clowning. He was not worried by the failure of his first road tour, nor by the authoritative opinions of his more experienced colleagues, who considered him an absolute mediocrity.

If we look back to the early days of Karandash's career it will become evident that

What a calamity! It must be put back together again

Everything was hopelessly confused:

now what goes on top of what?

this failure, far from being accidental, was inevitable, it was even predestined.

Rumyantsev found it difficult to accept the traditional clown's mask of buffoonery. He rebelled at the traditional "red-headed" clown's standard assortment of time-tested tricks and witticisms.

He could not accept the old, but the new had not yet evolved, it had not yet been born into the Soviet circus of the time.

The clown in the ring.... Who was that hideously painted man in the disgusting wig and foolish coat? Who was he? What country did he come from, what part of society did he represent? Who was he making fun of?

If, in the circus of pre-revolutionary times, some details of the clown's costume were a parody on existing styles (such as his tremendous shoes) or at one time his manner (brash and sly) could be regarded as an exaggerated satire on the vulgarity of the philistines, the very first years of the Soviet circus brought this type of clowning to a crisis, to a dead end in which the reliable buffoon now found himself stranded.

At the sight of a park attendant, he decided to take the statue's place

What a success! But now he didn't want to get down

The impostor had to be removed bodily

Then he decided to try his luck in the circus. No one was angry with him here

The social values of the new Soviet society had changed beyond recognition. Life was taking a new course and the time-honoured targets of the clown's jokes—the small merchants, idlers, dandies, etc.—vanished from the scene. However, the clown continued as before, he became mummified and lost his touch as a satirical impersonation.

In search of a new means of expression clowns began copying such popular foreign film comedians as Pat and Pataschon and Charlie Chaplin.

Rumyantsev, too, tried his hand at this and became one of Charlie Chaplin's many impersonators

One should note that Charlie Chaplin (this was during the early 30s) was as yet unknown to the Soviet public as the creator of the famous *City Lights* and *New Times*, in which the truly humane nature of his great talent as a comedian comes through with tremendous force.

Rumyantsev only knew of Chaplin's early short comedies. Thus, in his impersonation he brought to the circus the eccentricity of Chaplin's costume, manner and behaviour. And that is why this impersonation was short-lived. He decided against continuing it during his very first season with the Leningrad Circus.

Rumyantsev was searching for something new, for something that would be his alone. He

This cross between a donkey and a bicycle is the latest word in modern vehicles

realised that imitation would be a block to his creative powers, that the new must arise from an image as humane as Chaplin's, but one suggested by Soviet reality. It had to be familiar to the audience, it had to be comprehensible.

Chaplin's traditional cane and bowler hat were shelved as there began a gradual evolution of a new costume, a new personality.

The result was Karandash.

Karandash! This new type of clown won his place in the Soviet circus in an amazingly short time.

Here was a merry little man in a baggy suit, with a coat that obviously had once belonged to someone else. Against a circus background, lost among strong, courageous, athletic men and women, his appearance was still more comical and helpless, he even seemed smaller than he actually was.

And when the little man reveals his common sense, skill and resourcefulness in his funny skits, the audience cannot but help laughing. When Karandash succeeds in fooling and out-witting his "enemies" (the m.c. or attendants) this is a victory of the meek over the bold, and the audience is quite naturally on his side.

The personality Karandash has created is both realistic and truthful. The circus has its

Even when Karandash isn't doing anything special, he still delights his audiences

Satire means washing off accumulated dirt

own special logic, its own special truth, and this is the truth of the absurd.

When, for instance, Karandash rides into the ring on a little donkey with an automobile licence plate suspended from its rump and begins "pumping up" the donkey's leg with a bicycle pump it is really absurd. But therein lies the truth of the absurd, for the audience is quite willing to believe that Karandash could not do otherwise. There is such true conviction in what he does, his gestures are so realistic, one cannot help but believe him and, therefore, laugh.

In one skit Karandash shoots a cucumber from a cannon, aiming it at someone in the audience who has tossed a ball back awkwardly to him. Silly? Yes, but the fuming Karandash could only have done as he did.

This then is the truth of the created image, the circus truth of buffoonery, absurdity!

In another skit Karandash, while strolling in a park, accidentally smashes a statue to bits. He tries to put Venus together again from the various chunks but is unsuccessful. He confuses the parts of her anatomy beyond all recall, creating ever new, extremely comical combinations. While the audience laughs at this funny skit, it sincerely commiserates with Karandash, who has got himself into such a mess.

In his best skits and witticisms Karandash has always remained faithful to the truth, though expressing it through his buffoonery.

There was a new note in Karandash's art during the war years. The funny skits were replaced by biting, pointed satire aimed at the enemies of his Motherland. This was not only a new approach, it was a much more difficult one, since the very image he had created was the least suitable one for presenting serious political themes.

Karandash solved this problem successfully, retaining both his established style and manner while presenting his own interpretations of the subjects that were uppermost in the minds of all Soviet people during the war years. He was still the same old Karandash, but now he would start a game with the m.c., or the audience. In his naïve, childish way he would ask if anyone wanted to see a skit he had made up.

"Do you want to see how the fascists advanced towards Moscow and then ran back again?"

66

His best trophy is the
bureaucrat's briefcase

And he would commence to change his clothes right in the ring, assuming the appearance of the personage he had chosen as his target. Then the skit would continue as a child's game, improvised right before the audience's eyes. Thus, Karandash remained himself in any disguise.

We see him as a fascist, as a woebegone, would-be conqueror of Moscow.

We see him as Adolph Hitler.

In his most successful skits Karandash created colourful, memorable images that viewed with the best political cartoons of the time.

Everything was carefully planned: every detail of his costume, every element of staging, each simplicity in itself and strictly within the bounds of the style and personality Karandash had created.

Thus, he attained his true maturity.

In one of his popular skits a fascist tank rolled into the ring. It was really only a barrel on wheels, with a swastika and a skull and cross-bones painted on the side. Karandash donned a tin pot for a helmet and picked up an axe and a club. What a lout he was! He clambered into the tank and rolled forward, shouting: *"Nach Moskau!"*

Bang! And the tank fell to pieces. Karandash barely managed to crawl out from under the wreckage and hobble off at top speed on a pair of crutches.

This simple skit was always greeted with laughter, both in the circus ring and on the many makeshift Army stages, for Karandash was a frequent and beloved performer for the troops at the front.

In another very successful wartime satire Karandash appeared in the ring carrying a small podium, a microphone and huge briefcase. After setting up the props, he would pull

his dog Pushok from the briefcase. Pushok, in a manner common to orators, would rest a paw on the podium and bark long and loud into the microphone. When he was through, Karandash would stuff him back into the briefcase and announce:

"You have just been listening to a speech by Herr Goebbels, Minister of Propaganda!"

Here, in a well-aimed satirical portrait, he found the right solution to an important political theme while remaining true to himself, for never once did he overstep the boundaries of his personality or style.

His has been a long and difficult creative search, one which has taken him from the bright lights of the Moscow Circus to the front-line roads that wound through razed cities and towns; from being the pre-war happy-go-lucky Karandash, master of the kindly clown's jest, to becoming a satirist never afraid of tackling topical political themes close to the hearts of the Soviet people.

1958

KIO AND HIS PREDECESSORS

By Y. Dmitriyev

Any show that has a magician, be it a circus or a stage performance, is always immensely popular. This is understandable, for a good magician makes his audience participate in every trick he does. Audience participation is by no means limited to the two or three persons who get up and come forward when the magician calls for volunteers, chiefly because magicians, as no other performers, need an audience that is with them all the way.

I would like to offer a small digression here.

Many magazines have a special page devoted to riddles, chess and checkers problems, charades, rebuses and crossword puzzles. In the evenings there are whole families who gather round to solve these problems. Since this calls for a lot of "brainwork", there is always a feeling of excitement in doing them. That is why there are so many puzzle fans. The magician's tricks are very much similar to the above. After all, he asks the audience to solve his puzzle, saying, for example: "Here, Ladies and Gentlemen, you see an empty crate, made of removable boards. Now watch me carefully as I throw this cloth over the box." In a moment he whisks off the cloth, and, lo and behold, there are three people standing inside the box! Where could they have come from? Well, try and guess. Use your brains, as the saying goes.

The act of any good magician is always a game he plays with the audience. He gives us riddles to solve and we try our best to do so. I believe that a magician's greatest merit lies in his ability to capture the attention of the audience and make it participate, quite voluntarily and with pleasure, in the proceedings. This is his incentive for creating ever new and interesting tricks, because the more intriguing they are, the more fun his game with the audience will be.

What is the origin of magic tricks? How have they found their way into the circus arena and the variety show? The history of magic* reaches far back into the past, to the times

* There are two types of magicians: the illusionists, who make use of various props for their tricks (mechanical devices, mirrors, trap-doors) and the manipulators (prestidigitators), whose tricks are based solely on sleight of hand, on the lightning-quick use of their fingers.

Presenting Kio, a master magician

of Ancient Egypt, where the high priests stunned the faithful with peals of thunder breaking within the temple walls, with statues that "wept" tears of milk. Naturally, the priests used simple conjuring tricks to achieve their astounding effects, just as in a later day priests of the church made use of them to create such miracles as "weeping" icons or the shrivelling Host. However, all these experiments usually remained within the church walls and had no influence on the development of conjuring as a form of entertainment.

As such it is associated with the evolution of science and takes its beginning in the latter part of the 18th century, i.e., at the time of the great discoveries in all fields of knowledge.

The first magicians usually demonstrated the latest technical discoveries, trying to produce the greatest possible visual effect on their audiences. Public interest grew in proportion to the development of scientific thought, especially so after the French Revolution.

It is interesting to note that in the 19th century magicians did not try to stress the mysterious nature of their tricks. On the contrary, they presented them to the accompaniment of a running commentary of light banter. In the 20th century, however, when bourgeois intellectuals became interested in mysticism and spiritualism, many conjurers enveloped themselves in a shroud of mystery, hinting that they had ties with the "supernatural" or that they had inherited their powers from the Hindu fakirs and the Egyptian magi.

In the 18th and 19th centuries the performers were mostly deft mechanics who demonstrated their cleverly built contraptions. One of them was a mechanic by the name of Pierre Dumoulin who came to Moscow in 1759. He took up residence in the German Quarter, in the house of Dame Nechet, where he demonstrated a small mechanical peasant woman of Berne who wove cloth, a deck of moving cards and an electrical machine.

In 1762, two miners exhibited a model of a machine that worked in a mine.

Far into the 19th century many magicians continued to show the latest scientific developments on the stage. Thus, a magician named Dablair exhibited, among other items, a microscope "in which animals that inhabit a drop of water seemed like giants." During his second visit to Russia Dablair advertised his performances as "Experiments in popular physics, natural magic and mechanics."

There are any number of similar examples. However, in their desire to astound and baffle their audiences, magicians soon discarded their old methods of simply demonstrating various contraptions and mechanisms. They wanted their audiences to ponder over the technique of their presentation and as yet felt no need to shroud their performances in mystery.

Bosco (Bartholomeo, 1792-1863) was one of the very popular magicians of the time. His Russian tour was a great success. One of his tricks consisted of the following: he would take a hen, put it in a cage, hang the cage from a nail on the wall and shoot it. Then he would pluck the fowl, put it in a pot, cover the pot with a lid and set it on a fire. When he removed the lid a live hen would emerge from the pot.

In another of his tricks he would take a kerchief from someone in the audience, place it on a little table and cover it with a cap. The next moment the kerchief would be found in a box on the opposite side of the stage or in the very same bottle from which Bosco had just poured himself a glass of wine. When he finally removed the cap from the table, a live rabbit would hop out from under it.

Another of his sensational tricks had twelve soldiers shooting at him, with volunteers from the audience loading the rifles. Bosco, unhurt, would dramatically catch the bullets on a little plate.*

Withal, he never assumed an air of mystery in any of his performances. As one reviewer of the time wrote: "He is not a fake, nor does he attribute his tricks to any supernatural force."

Dablair performed in a similar vein. His most popular trick consisted of the following: he would fire a pistol, and at the sound of the shot dozens of candles placed all over the stage, on tables and in the chandeliers would light up.

Friquel was another of the many magicians who toured Russia in the 19th century. One of his tricks was to take a

* However, the rifles were loaded from the muzzle and Bosco drove the bullets in with a specially-made ramrod. The bullets entered the ramrod and he then removed them.

73

The art of illusion is that of producing something where there was nothing

*If you don't believe this is a real
lion, try getting into the cage*

sheet of paper, tear it to bits, put the bits into a top hat and pull out a long paper ribbon.

The famous magician Alexandre Herman began his Petersburg tour in 1852. He was an elegant, charming and witty young man who spoke many languages. The stage would be set with nothing but three tables, a large one in the middle and two smaller ones on the sides. Herman would take a roast chicken, tear it in two and produce a live fowl from each half; he would place a rabbit on one of the smaller tables and cover it with a hat. When he removed the hat it would reveal an entire rabbit family underneath. Herman was the first to present a trick called "The Floating Boy" in which a boy would lean his elbow on a stick and hang suspended in the air, parallel to the floor and even fall asleep in this position. "The Bountiful Bottle" was another sensational trick. Herman would pour drink after drink for the audience, from lemonade to champagne, and all from one and the same bottle.

This list of magicians could be expanded greatly. All of them performed their tricks to the accompaniment of a running commentary of jokes and witticisms, and the entire performance was given in a relaxed and merry mood. The press of the time never failed to note the difference between these magicians and witch-doctors and sorcerers.

Things took a very different turn at the beginning of the 20th century, when the majority of magicians appeared as Hindu fakirs, Chinese sorcerers and spiritualists and their performances took on an ever-increasing air of mysticism. The following example will serve to illustrate this point.

Okito (Theodore Bambourg), a conjurer, toured the U.S.S.R. twice, once in the 20s, and once in the 30s. The highlight of his act was called "The Mysterious Ball." The stage was plunged into nearly total darkness (this was a necessary step from a technical point as well, for otherwise the audience would have noticed the strings Okito manipulated to direct the movements of the ball). The musical accompaniment was very sinister. Two helpers, gliding soundlessly across the stage, would carry out a large and apparently very heavy crate which they then placed on a table. Okito, made up like a Japanese and wearing a kimono, would suddenly appear. Standing at a considerable distance from the crate and slowly raising his hands with fingers that seemed unnaturally long, he would cause the lid to rise and a bronze ball to float out of the crate. It soared over the stage, following the movements of his hands. Finally, it would fall back into the crate and the lid would come crashing down.

Naturally, the audience knew that this was a trick, but the magician himself tried to prove in every possible way that what he did was accomplished through his supernatural powers.

Many other magicians chose this form of presentation. "Two performances only!" read a 1910 playbill. "Madame Everini, Performer of Magic and Egyptian Mysteries and Grignon de Benoit, Sorcerer."

Fakirs became immensely popular in the early 20th century. Most bourgeois intellectuals evinced an avid interest in the occult and in man's ecstatic being as the true expression of his "mystic soul."

Obviously, the circus "fakirs" had nothing whatsoever to do with India. Thus, *Theatrical Day*, in one of its 1909 issues, disclosed the fact that Nan Sahib, the well-known circus fakir, was none other than a Russian peasant by the name of Karlinsky.

The "fakirs" stuck pins in their hands and tongues, nailed their tongues to boards and bit off pieces of red-hot iron. The so-called Egyptian magi were their next of kin. One such, Ali, would smoke a dozen cigarettes without exhaling the smoke; he swallowed frogs, goldfish and salamanders and then spit them back into a tank. He drank kerosene and breathed fire.

The wizard Amos announced in the papers that he would "sew up his mouth and still his heart." He invited all those who were interested in the occult to witness his feat.

There were also "living corpses". Here is an excerpt from a newspaper of the times: "Caspardi is a living corpse. His nose and mouth are stuffed with cotton wool, a large tampon is forced down his throat, then his nose, mouth and eyes are covered with plaster and his head is swathed in scarves. He is placed in a glass box, lowered into a grave and buried under sand and earth. Caspardi spends 14 minutes in the grave and is then revived with ether."

"Fakirs" and "magi" appeared in many bourgeois circuses. Their acts were a disgrace to human dignity and were based on mysticism and various freakish qualities; in a word, they

There are very few people, indeed, who can produce a beautiful woman from thin air

were an insult to the very essence of the circus, where the skill and beauty of the human body are celebrated. These performers were actually freaks, playing on the basest instincts of the gawking crowd.

I have digressed into the history of magic, because I think it is interesting and even necessary to explain what E. F. Kio, the Soviet magician, encountered when he made his circus debut, the traditions he furthered and those he had to overcome, for by then the world of magic and magicians had come a far way upon a long, uneven road.

And so, at the time Kio made his debut magicians had had a good many years of experience. There were famous magicians, interesting tricks had been invented and sleight of hand had been developed to a fine point. The best of the magicians based their knowledge on scientific facts, and their acts were both funny and interesting. In time, however, these magicians displayed a tendency to envelop both themselves and their experiments in a cloud of mystery.

Kio, while continuing in the best traditions of his predecessors, openly revolted against the legacy of the various magi and fakirs. He felt the tricks must be interesting to begin with and especially stressed this fact, thus dispelling once and for all the aura of mystery attached to the magician's art.

Kio was the first magician in the world to appear solely in circus arenas. To a great extent this was responsible for the heightened effect of his act, it deprived him of the all-saving curtains and made it much more difficult for him to perform his tricks. Kio had to change all the old tricks accordingly and take the new dimensions of the circus arena into account when staging his new tricks. Among the many he invented are "The Burning Woman," "Trolley-Car," "The Phone Booth Vanishing Act" and others. All these tricks are staged in the centre of the ring. Numerous tricks invented and first performed by Kio are now part of the repertoire of most magicians.

Kio is a very bold creator, he is not afraid of taking risks or of blazing new paths if the artistic effect of his act is heightened.

Kio's billing once announced that he would appear with seventy-five assistants. True enough, he was surrounded by endless helpers in the ring. They not only had a "decorative effect," but were a sort of stage curtain around him, conceal-ing, when necessary, things he did not want the audience to see. There was much too much affectation in this needlessly large entourage and needless pomposity, and both the public and the press reacted to it ironically.

In 1947, Kio was to have begun his Moscow tour. At the time I worked at the Main Circus Office and remember how the question of his assistants was brought up again.

"I'll have a hard time without them," Kio had said. "And won't the act seem skimpy? All right, let's try it your way!"

And so Kio did away with all but the most necessary of his helpers.

It would seem to be a minor point, but anyone who has ever had anything to do with magicians knows how difficult it is for them to deviate from their established style and back-drops, for this usually means reconstructing the entire act.

Here is a more telling example. Kio often changes his act (by comparison, the majority of magicians perform the same tricks for decades). What does a magician's première entail? It means the invention of new tricks and the designing and manufacturing of new props. This is always an experiment, for who can tell whether the new tricks will be a success? What if the audience sees through them too quickly? Kio, for one, was never afraid of this possibility and invented not only new tricks but entirely new acts as well.

One does not simply invent a new trick. It must be staged in a way to intrigue and fascinate the audience. Kio was the first of the magicians to employ a producer and set designer, to seek a new approach and strive towards a maximum of expression in the presentation of his tricks. His programmes included traditional and carnival tricks, comic sketches and small skits. Kio usually talks during his performance. His assistants are clowns, acrobats and dancers, and that is why he calls the whole a magical review. Kio had broadened our concept not only of the possibilities afforded the art of magic but also of the way in which tricks can be presented.

It is interesting to note that he is always ready to participate in other spheres. Anyone who has attended a performance of Mayakovsky's play *The Bedbug* at the Mayakovsky Theatre has probably noticed in the programme credits that the various magic tricks performed in the play were staged by Kio. In an article for *Moskovsky Komsomolets* Kio described in detail popular magic suitable for youth festivals.

One must be more than an inventor to be a magician, one must also be a very good organiser. Kio's talent as an organiser comes to the fore in his work in the ring and with his assistants when creating a new act.

The latter is a difficult undertaking involving many persons. It is to Kio's credit that the producers, actors, composers, engineers, directors of the factories where the props are made and the workers who make them all have a lively interest in the new act. Anyone who has ever worked with Kio falls under the spell of his charm, his energy, his desire to make the act as interesting as possible, his conviction that what he is doing will be of value to great masses of people. Inertia, boredom and indifference are unknown to Kio and his troupe.

M. Marches, Cleo Dorotti, A. Shag and the recently retired A. Vadimov (Ali-Vad) are but several of our excellent circus magicians. However, none of them has ever enjoyed Kio's popularity. His talent as an organiser was probably a decisive factor in this respect.

Kio has close to thirty performers in his act, some of whom appear on stage and others who do not. However, the success of any given trick depends on each and every one of them, on the tempo in which the trick is performed, on its effect and on seeing to it that the audience never guesses how it is done. The work of Kio's assistants can best be compared with the working of a well-oiled clock. Everything is planned, down to the last second, a fact one can check easily enough by standing backstage with a stopwatch. Withal, there is never any bustle or commotion, no one speaks, for each knows his job and his exact place. While one prop is on stage another stands ready behind the curtain, a third is nearly ready, a fourth is being readied and a fifth is being moved closer to the entrance. That is why there is never even a second's pause between Kio's tricks. However, one never has the sensation that a trick is being rushed offstage to make way for the next one. If you try to imagine this menagerie of people, props, birds and animals you will understand how difficult it is to achieve perfect harmony in this seeming confusion. The majority of magicians never seem to achieve such conciseness and organisation in their performances.

More important still, a real magician must also be a good actor. Kio, for one, is a talented actor. He is rather handsome and has great charm. If he had chosen the theatre as his career he would undoubtedly have been a leading man. Kio's stage manner is very dignified. There is a slight hoarseness to his voice, but his diction is clear, his words are simple and, what is most important, he says only enough to prepare the audience for the next trick or to comment on the one he is performing.

Kio's greatest asset as an actor is his slightly ironic manner in regard to his own magic. It is in the hint of a smile on his lips, in the familiar way he raps on his mysterious boxes and props, and in the fact that he is always ready to include one or several clowns in his act. His manner and appearance seem to say: "I have thought up several startling and interesting puzzles for you. Now try and find the solutions. There is nothing mysterious about anything I will do, but it will take a bit of brainwork to solve these puzzles."

This approach has produced a number of skits based on everyday life, which is probably why they are so popular.

One of these involves two telephone booths which are set up at opposite sides of the ring. A number of people enter them and in some mysterious way disappear, only to reappear at the opposite side of the ring. There are a mother and daughter, an elegant lady, a dandy and many other types. The poor clown standing nearby is completely confused by all this coming and going and cannot for the world of him understand what is happening.

Such an "everyday" approach to magic-making dispels once and for all any trace of mysticism, it increases the audience's interest immensely, for when one presents "mysterious trunks", or "Pharaoh's vases", the very objects chosen cast a shadow of mystery over the audience. Here, however, they see two very ordinary telephone booths, the kind they have phoned from innumerable times. And then, quite suddenly, people go into them and disappear. How is it done? This, truly, is a cause for wonder.

Kio realises that today's audiences are so technically advanced as to readily see through a trick, and that is why he makes use of comic tricks, and why, more often than not, people take part in his tricks.

82

How in the world could the men we have just seen heading towards the outer lobby suddenly appear in the empty carriage standing in the middle of the ring? Here is another brain-teaser. We are confronted with the magician's ingenuity as well as with his excellent technique.

How does Kio perform his tricks? In order to achieve the desired effect he often distracts the audience. But then, why should we give him away? If you know how his tricks are done they won't seem interesting any more, and some might even say: "Oh, so that's how he does it! Why, there's nothing to it at all!"

Well, dear readers, you will have to guess the answers yourselves. I doubt whether you'll be very successful though, for Kio is a magician, and he will make you concentrate all of your attention exactly where he wants it. I hope you won't think he's a hypnotist. The simple answer is that Kio is a top-rate magician.

1958

SERGE-ALEXANDROV

By E. Krolle
and Y. Lennik

On a rainy November day in Tiflis in 1892 the wind tore at a circus playbill announcing: "Sergei-Serge, Trapeze Artist."

The Tiflis Circus was jammed. An infant's wail backstage was drowned in the thunder of applause. This was the first news the circus troupe had of Sergei-Serge's newborn son Alexander.

Yes, Alexander Serge was born in a circus. No wonder he began his circus career at an early age. Alexander was only five when he made his debut, doing simple acrobatic tricks with the clowns. At the age of nine he became an acrobat, performing also with Kosta's Bicycle Riders. By the time he was fifteen, he was a solo bareback rider, but his imagination was fired by his desire to stage his own horse act.

The scene changes to the city of Ufa. Here was Alexander's first horse, bought with his own hard-earned money. However, his dream remained a dream, for the First World War broke out. Serge was called up.

The eighteen-year-old youth in the army greatcoat still had his heart set on the circus. Soon he began appearing in an act at the People's House Gardens and Petrovsky Island in Petrograd.

Serge-Alexandrov, a once famous circus rider, wields his trainer's baton as a true conductor

The February Revolution brought the workers and peasants neither peace, nor land, nor bread. The circus arena became the site of crowded political meetings, and the circus performers were now the ever-present witnesses at these heated gatherings. After the lights had been turned off in the smoke-filled arena, they would stay on into the night, arguing about current events. These meetings often took place in the Modern Circus in Petrograd. Here Serge first heard Lenin speak.

The theatres and circuses were nationalised after the October Revolution, and the performers themselves became the full masters of the Petrograd Circus.

Serge threw himself into his work. He tried his hand at every type of circus performance, he took part in drawing up the programmes, in directing the acts and was busy in civic affairs.

In January 1920, the Theatre of Popular Comedy was inaugurated in the Iron Hall of the Petrograd People's House. Serge, who was enamoured of the theatre, eventually found his way to the producer, S. Radlov. He was taken on and was extremely successful in the role of an old crone pursuing a sailor in love with her granddaughter. Besides participating in a series of comic scenes, Serge was to jump from

One off, two to go!

the top storey of a house. During this leap, which was extremely well done, he resembled an Olympic champion more than an old woman.

The next production, after the play closed, was a circus and variety show in which Serge appeared as a bareback rider. Standing astride a galloping horse he did a somersault through paper hoops, landing on his feet. The high point of this programme was entitled "The Four Devils." Serge, playing the daredevil, would climb to the top of the circus cupola, blindfold himself and leap headlong into a net far below. Konstantin Derzhavin, a well-known critic, wrote: "To the thunderous applause of the audience this man with springs instead of muscles would come forth with ever new acrobatic feats."

In February 1920, Maxim Gorky visited the Theatre of Popular Comedy and wrote several one-act comedies especially for the troupe. Once, when the performers had gathered at his house on Kronverksky Prospekt, Gorky said:

"I like the circus. It's real work. You are not performing. You are working."

After the theatre closed, Serge and Taurek, a fellow acrobat, put together a comical act which they presented at variety shows, on outdoor stages and in summer theatres.

Forte!

The tempo increases

The drums roll and everyone holds his breath

At the time, there were very few horse acts in Soviet circus programmes, and Serge decided to return to the circus and to riding. In one of his acts he leaped over seven horses or twenty men.

At an exhibition of jumpers in Kiev, in 1924, Serge met with Sobolevsky and Armando, the greatest men in the field, but it was he who took first place in the contest. This gave him the idea to create a troupe of circus riders.

In putting the act together Serge displayed unusual imagination and talent as a producer. In time the act acquired its well-known compositional unity, breath-taking pace and beauty. The most difficult tricks pass before us in rapid succession as the riders go through a series of acrobatic tricks on several horses. Serge is the creator of a unique, new school of circus riding and is far ahead of the better-known foreign circus riders, even such famous ones as Frediani, Cozzi and Vincenzo.

During one of his performances Serge slipped and fell from a galloping horse, breaking his knee-cap.

"Well, it's not as bad as breaking your head," he said philosophically. From then on he devoted most of his time to training young riders, but also took part in two pantomimes, "The Black Pirate" and "Moscow in Flames."

Serge has remained one of the most devoted advocates of bareback riding and has passed this love on to his sons.

On an autumn evening in 1941, when Moscow was deep in a war-time blackout and searchlights crossed and recrossed in the threatening sky, passers-by were few and far between. But a large and lively crowd was gathering at the circus entrance on Tsvetnoi Boulevard. There were many men in uniform in the crowd.

The posters outside the circus read:

"A Theatrical Prologue and Parade, Staged by A. S. Alexandrov-Serge. Merited Artiste of the R.S.F.S.R."

Soon Serge got together a circus troupe that entertained the soldiers of the Western Front. Their arena was usually a camouflaged forest clearing close to the front-lines and the programme was made up of the best and funniest acts.

Serge has a treasured scrapbook of clippings from army newspapers with reviews of his performances.

88

Towards the end of 1944, Serge founded a riding and acrobatic studio at the Ivanovo Circus. There were to be nine boys and three girls ranging in age from 12 to 14 in his first class. But so many hopefuls applied that he could have had a squadron. However, only seventy of the five hundred applicants gave any hope of remaining in the saddle for more than five minutes.

The days passed. The children chosen for the group had lessons in gymnastics, classical and modern dancing, the history of circus art and, finally, bareback riding. Now they were much more sure of themselves in the saddle. True, of the seventy who had been taken on probation, only twelve remained after a month of training.

And then it was time for their first test, for their first public appearance at the Fourth All-Union Review of Circus Performers.

This first performance was a triumph. The audience was captivated by the precise and lively act, by the feeling of sportsmanship that was the core of their performance. The young riders displayed an excellent technique and true skill. They performed the most difficult of somersaults on horseback.

And then came the highlight of the act.

A galloping horse rode round and round the ring. In a flash, nine boys and three girls leaped to its back. There was such lightness and ease in what they had done that one might easily have imagined it was a log on the ground, not a galloping horse. And their smiles, their young, happy smiles could charm any audience.

The war ended. Serge's sons, Yuri and Svyatoslav, who had been through the war from Moscow to Berlin now returned home, bringing back twelve military orders and medals to their circus family. They had seen their share of fighting and had also performed for their comrades-in-arms whenever there had been a pause between battles.

When Svyatoslav and Yuri returned to the circus they began preparing for the Fifth All-Union Review of Circus Performers.

Floodlights lit up the arena. A fanfare of trumpets announced the appearance of the bareback riders. Horses galloped round the ring with riders standing upright on their backs, unsaddling them without ever slackening their speed.

Serge-Alexandrov's riders know
what audience appeal is

The tempo increased. Seven lithe and powerful youths and a pretty girl seemed to compete in skill as they leaped to the horses' backs and performed their daredevil tricks, doing forward and backward somersaults as they jumped down to the arena again. Each trick was more amazing than the previous one.

Next to appear in the ring was Synok, Alexandrov's favourite horse. Four riders stood in the centre of the ring. With a swift running jump they all leaped to the horse's back and were standing on the galloping horse a moment later. This trick has never been attempted before.

The applause had barely died down when a new trick began. A rider stood on a galloping horse with a second rider on his shoulders. Suddenly, the top man bent over in a somersault and came to his feet in front of the bottom man. In another variation of this trick he did a backward somersault, coming to his feet in his partner's place, while the bottom man of the act leaped to the ground. This trick only takes a few seconds to perform and seems simplicity itself, but months and years of persistent training and rehearsals went into it.

Serge's troupe first went on a foreign tour in 1919. Their Warsaw engagement was a great success, and when it officially ended the crowds continued to pour in to see them. Serge and his riders stayed on a month and a half longer than called for the terms of their contract. After their return to Moscow they went on tour once again. This was a triumphant tour of Belgium, France and England.

Everywhere they appeared, in Brussels, Antwerp, Paris, Lyons and Saint-Etiènne, they were greeted by applause, flowers and crowds. Once, when the entire ring was covered with a carpet of live flowers, Serge bent down and from among them picked a small bouquet of forget-me-nots. Who was the unknown friend who had brought back memories of his faraway homeland, of his friends and the birch-trees of Moscow?

Next came Manchester and London. Though the British public met them warmly, there was still, at the beginning, a feeling of tenseness and curiosity towards the Russians. However, after the very first performances the Soviet riders won the hearts of their audiences. Serge became one of their favourites, and even the most sceptical of circus-goers were enthralled.

There followed dozens of other foreign cities, hundreds of performances.

The days flew by, and the years. Was it not time to take a rest? But was there any time for rest? Serge dreamed of staging a Russian bareback act with daredevil riding, an accordion and a spirited troika.

The scene is the Leningrad Circus during a rehearsal. There are no sets, no audience, no dignified m.c. No one but the other circus performers, the first and most severe critics of any new act.

The talk quieted down as the sound of a Russian accordion filled the arena. It was joined by balalaikas, shepherd's pipes and a tambourine.

A Russian troika came galloping into the ring. The riders were dressed in sheepskin coats and hats. Serge sat in the driver's seat. There was such gaiety and laughter, it was so characteristic of the Russian people, that one could not help smiling with them.

The performers threw off their heavy coats and turned into acrobats. What was it that was so familiar and exciting about their act? Why, everything was based on traditional Russian games! The sturdy young riders seemed to be competing in skill. There was not a moment's pause, not a moment's rest, the pace was quick, the pace was everything.

Serge, the strong-willed manager, took his place in the centre of the ring. In response to a barely perceptible flick of his stick the act commenced. Several riders performed acrobatic tricks on horseback. The drums rolled, heralding a difficult moment, a backward somersault. Both Serge and the performers tensed, for this was a test of their skill. Two horses galloped evenly round the ring. Two riders, one standing on the other's shoulders, were on the lead horse. Victor, the top man, braced himself and went into a swift backward somersault, coming to his feet on the second horse as it galloped under him.

A sigh of relief passed through the crowd. Everyone present, the performers, producers, attendants and musicians, applauded and congratulated Serge. Something he had been thinking

92

about and working on for so long had passed in review in a matter of seconds.

Serge was always a hard task-master, both in regard to his own performances and to his students. "I remember once Victor was rehearsing his backward somersault and Slava was the bottom man," he said. "They started out fine, but Victor just couldn't manage to land on the horse's back as he came out of his somersault. He kept landing on its head or its tail. Then the horse would bolt, glaring at him and not understanding what it was expected to do. More often than not, though, he landed on the ground with a bang. He discovered the law of gravity first-hand then, but he'd climb right back on Slava's shoulders and start from the beginning. Rehearsals usually ended with the horse shrugging its shoulders hopelessly and trotting off to the stable."

But rehearsals continued day after day until finally all was letter-perfect.

Serge-Alexandrov, Merited Artiste of the R.S.F.S.R., has come a long way and accomplished much. His artistic achievements have brought him many government awards.

This wonderful master of the circus is always ready to share his knowledge and skill with the coming generation of circus performers who are now carrying on the best traditions of bareback riding.

1961

ALI-BEK
KANTEMIROV

By V. Angarsky
and A. Viktorov

Two Caucasians carry a large white paper hoop into the ring. The lettering on it reads: "Ali-Bek Kantemirov." There is a sound of horse's hooves and in another second a white horse and rider come flying through the hoop. When they come to a halt we see the rider's white hat and white coat and the face of a middle-aged man. But this is the face of a virile, powerful, strong-willed man. If one does not know beforehand, one would never guess that this swift rider is over eighty, with a long and eventful life behind him.

Ali-Bek Kantemirov began his circus career in Malugin's Circus in the Northern Caucasus. The year was 1906. Kantemirov had a poverty-ridden childhood, he spent six years working at a brick factory and four years as a jockey in the various hippodromes of the Caucasus. He was strong and tall and known for his skill in riding competitions and games. But his type of riding was something new for the circus and the manager was doubtful whether the public would like him. Ali-Bek was quite certain that the kind of riding he loved so much would be a success and did not waste time trying to convince the manager. Instead, he began rehearsing. Two months later, on February 11, 1907, he made his debut in Batumi, performing a dance with daggers, jumping his horse over obstacles and barriers and displaying a high class of riding. Thus, Ali-Bek became a circus performer. He spent a great deal of time and energy creating new and unusual tricks. Until then a *djigit** performance meant exotic dances and shooting accompanied by guttural cries. Kantemirov would slip out of the saddle at full gallop, slide under the horse's belly and come up on the other side. Then he would climb over the horse's neck and between its front legs at full gallop or fire a pistol at a target while standing on one hand on the saddle. These were such unusual tricks that Ali-Bek soon became known throughout Russia. He toured Austria-Hungary in 1908 and again in 1914. Though riding was extremely popular in Russia and Austria-Hungary, no one had seen the likes of his daring tricks before.

It is typical of Ali-Bek that success has never stood in the way of his further perfecting his skill. He planned to create

---

* *Djigit*—skilled horseman.

Ali-Bek's riders are at home on any horse or carriage

Blindfolded riding makes every-one sit up and take notice

a troupe of riders but lacked the necessary funds and so continued his act solo. After the Revolution, however, the state allocated the sum he needed and Ali-Bek set out for his native Ossetia, bringing back a group of *djigits* and horses. He taught them his technique and together they presented a new act. The search for new tricks and new skits continued. Ali-Bek included trick riding, acrobatics on a cart and the music and dances of the Caucasus in his act. The troupe toured Germany in 1927, appearing in the circuses of Carl Hagenbeck, Sarrasani, Médrano and Willie Schumann. Ali-Bek and his riders spent three triumphant years in Germany, returning to the Soviet Union in 1931. The next twenty-five years flew by in touring the circuses of the Soviet Union. Ali-Bek went on a return tour of France in 1957 and Henry Thétard, the French circus historian, wrote: "An act I saw as a young man at Sarrasani's now, in my old age, I see in Paris. Ali-Bek is as magnificent as ever." None of Ali-Bek's original *djigits* were in the troupe by then. He had taught them his skill and they had gone on to found their own acts. But Ali-Bek never remained alone. He took on a new group of *djigits* and trained them and when they, in turn, went on to other circuses, he formed still another group. In all, Ali-Bek has trained some 120 circus riders. The most famous of them is Tuganov, People's Artiste of the R.S.F.S.R.

At present, three of Ali-Bek's sons are in his troupe. This is not merely a family tradition. His sons have all gone through his school of riding and have passed the most severe tests. Hasan-Bek is as dedicated to riding as his father. He is a graduate of the Institute of Physical Culture and is now enrolled in the Producing and Directing Department of the Moscow Theatrical Institute. Ir-Bek has been riding champion of the U.S.S.R. five times. Mukhtar-Bek, the youngest, is interested in field and track athletics. Recently both Hasan-Bek and Ir-Bek were awarded the title of Merited Artistes of the North-Ossetian Autonomous Republic.

Ali-Bek and his sons are now appearing with a new programme of riding games of the peoples of the U.S.S.R. These include, among others, *Tsvkhen-Burti*, a Georgian game, *Ogdarysh*, a Kirghiz riders' wrestling game, a traditional cavalry game, and the dance of a *djigit* and his horse.

Ali-Bek and his riders have taken part in such films as *Dangerous Paths, Identity Known, Ataman Kodr,* and *Courageous Men*, in which he has performed the most hair-raising stunts. His boundless energy has never faltered, it has provided the drive behind his constant search for perfection.

1964

FOUR - LEGGED
PERFORMERS

By Boris Eder

In our childhood we have all read of the thrilling adventures of someone who has at one time or another saved a wild animal from death, only to find in it later a faithful friend.

Man has learned to tame animals, but it has taken many centuries for him to study the ways and nature of wild animals.

Wild beasts were first displayed in zoos. Now and then some daring young man would venture into a cage with them. In time, the presentation became more complex. The animals would see a man entering their cage holding a flaming torch or shooting blank cartridges at them. They would become panicky and cower in terror. The inherent dangers of this "terrifying act" would draw in the crowds, and the zoo owners, whose motive was nothing more commendable than profit, widely advertised the performances of the first animal-tamers.

This "wild" style was soon taken up in the circus, and the more terrifying an act was, the more fire and shooting it included, the more ferociously the animals behaved, the more the managers valued it, especially in West-European circuses. Animal-tamers were often killed or maimed in the ring.

Zherebilov-Veyani, a Russian lion-tamer, believed that terror was the only means of keeping his lions submissive. For a while he managed to suppress their will, but he never succeeded in taming them. For a split second during a performance in Novocherkassk Zherebilov weakened the fear he held as a whip over the lions' heads and was instantly torn to bits.

Farukh, another lion-tamer, worked in the circuses of pre-revolutionary Russia. He was attacked several times and eventually left the circus. In the 30s he returned with a group of lions, but his methods were the same. Farukh's comeback was short-lived, for he was ripped apart during a performance in Bryansk.

However, such cases were very rare in Russia. A new school of animal-training, founded by Vladimir and Anatoly Durov, gained popularity throughout the world.

The basic principle of their method is a kindly attitude towards their animals. This is diametrically opposed to the old school, it means much less shooting, fire, terror and other superfluous and horrifying stage effects. Patient training, a love for animals and a truly humane attitude towards them has produced unheard-of results.

N. Gladilshchikov, one of the first Soviet animal-trainers, began his circus career with a performing bear, appearing at various fairs and circuses. After some years he presented a mixed group of animals. Lions, brown and polar bears and Great Danes performed together in a large enclosure.

I would like to mention our famous woman trainer, Irina Bugrimova. For many years circus audiences have come to see this graceful woman and the huge and beautiful lions that cater to her every wish. In 1955, Irina Bugrimova and her assistant, Konstantin Parmakyan, took on a group of eleven young lions that are now in their prime. She has her special friends among them, and they sometimes help her out in difficult situations. These fierce cats are attached to their mistress and are very obedient. Here is a story she told me: "It happened in Czechoslovakia when I was on tour there in 1958. I was sitting in my trailer dressing-room before the evening performance, pottering around, for we circus performers always have household chores to do. It was cosy inside and things were progressing nicely.

"It would soon be time for the show to go on, and I decided to lie down and rest. I set aside my work and went over to the window to have a look at the clearing where the lions' cages were. Just then the trailer door flew open. I spun around in time to see a man nearly falling into the room. He was as pale as a ghost. With one hand he was clawing at the door and pointing with the other. I could see he was trying to say something. Finally, I made out the word 'Lion!' A terrible scene flashed through my mind: someone was trapped in a cage with a lion! Suddenly, we heard a woman's piercing scream. I shoved the man aside and threw open the door.

"There, on a little hillock about five yards away, a huge lion was outlined against the setting sun. A light breeze rippled his mane. He was so magnificent that for a moment I forgot the danger which threatened others as I admired his beauty. My animals had never seemed as majestic and powerful in their cages or in the ring as he did now.

"There was shouting and the lion turned his head. In the next instant he had taken a giant leap.

" 'Demon!' I shouted as I recognised him.

"He was leaping about playfully, retreating farther and farther away. I realised that he was enjoying his taste of

Boris Eder knows who's king of the beasts

This is better than resting on your laurels

freedom. Then I heard my husband's voice. He was running towards the lion. At the sound of our voices Demon halted. He suddenly let out a roar in which I detected his dismay and, I thought, his plea for help.

"The cage in which my lions travel was rolled into the clearing. I walked towards Demon, calling his name softly. When he was convinced that it was really I, he trotted over. I took him by the mane and patted him gently as I headed towards the cage. The mighty beast walked alongside, pressing against my leg, as if seeking protection. Yet a moment before he had caused so many people to panic as he roamed about. They had screamed in terror, though they were all in their trailers and he could never have opened the doors himself.

"The door of the cage was raised and Demon darted inside. It was only then that I realised the danger that had been averted. Demon might have easily bumped into someone, he might have killed someone or might have been shot. Perhaps even I had been in danger, too. The only 'weapon' I had had was the cloth belt of my bathrobe. Other performers and attendants were running towards us from all directions.

" 'Don't worry, everything's under control now,' I said and tied my belt on.

"There in the cage was that beautiful beast, Demon. He was stretched out and I could see that he was happy, because he was home at last."

Yes, lions can be gentle and obedient. But at times their wild instincts are aroused, they become irritable and mean and have been known to attack their trainers. True, many are the times when a trainer has found a "helper" among his big cats. Here is something that happened to me in 1932, when I was appearing at the Ivanovo Circus with a group of lions.

It was springtime, when lions are more irritable and mean than ever. When I entered the cage during a rehearsal one day, Primus and Riffi attacked me, clawing me deeply. As I struggled with them I tried not to fall, for this would have been fatal. Suddenly Krym, the leader of the lion pack, jumped off his pedestal and ran around me from the back. "This is it," I thought. How mistaken I was! Krym threw himself upon my attackers, pressing them back, forcing them into a corner. This, as nothing else, proved that man and the king of the beasts could be friends.

In the circus arena we see a huge lion riding on the back of a galloping horse. What a magnificent and thrilling scene! One must remember that a lion never loses his carnivorous instincts, while a horse has an instinctive fear of lions. But both of them know that standing nearby is a human being who will prevent one of them from attacking and will always come to the aid of the other.

A. N. Buslayev, Merited Artiste of the R.S.F.S.R., has created a fascinating and effective act.

There is a short prologue in which horses perform in traditional manner. This is followed by the magnificent entrance of four lions and two Great Danes. At a sign from the trainer, Tamara Buslayeva, they take their places at a table, as if waiting for food to be brought in. And they are not mistaken. A clown enters, carrying a piece of meat. He walks around the table, teasing the animals, but not offering them any. Then, a live rooster is placed on the table. It walks about, right in front of the lions' maws. The lions sniff at it and lick their chops. Then the rooster is hoisted up under the circus top. The disappointed beasts follow his flight with their eyes. Now we come to the highlight of the act. The lions, "annoyed" at the rooster that has got away so easily, leap upon the horses and begin galloping around the ring. The audience is first paralysed and then amazed at the sight of the lion riders pressing close to the galloping steeds like true jockeys. The lions are calm and intent. The horses are restrained, with an infrequent snort or watchful eye, tell-tale signs that they are apprehensive of the animals crouching firmly on their backs.

In 1949, a new act was added to the programme of the Soviet circus. It was Valentin Filatov and his "Bear Circus," dispelling once and for all the old saying "as clumsy as a bear." Under the careful tutelage of their trainer, the big animals have mastered nearly every form of circus art. We see a bear standing on his front paws on a pedestal, tossing and spinning a cigar-shaped log with his hind paws, then twirling a long pole with flames on either end. Another bear is blindfolded and mounts two free-standing ladders where he does a one-handed handstand. There are bear tightrope-walkers, bear jugglers and the ever-popular boxing bears.

Bears on speeding motorcycles are the highlight of the programme. They switch the headlights on and off with an experienced touch of their paws, and a bear cub sits behind the driver, embracing him tightly. After circling the ring several times the motorcycle drivers exit.

This is a most unusual performance. So many patient hours of work went into this magnificent show and so much sugar was consumed by the bears during rehearsals! Filatov spoon-fed the cubs condensed milk for their good work.

104

Never before was there such an act anywhere in the world. However, Filatov was not content with what he had achieved and he continued teaching his animals new tricks. His success was due to his skill and patience in discovering the individual "talents" of his four-legged performers.

The circus has always been known for its excellent performing horses. Boris Maizhelli has been appearing with trained horses for

A woman always has the last word

over twenty years. The horses form a pyramid, they waltz and jump over a flaming obstacle. There are interesting and popular skits in which they "play" the roles of people. walking about on their hind legs, swinging on swings. In one. the arena is set with a table and chair and a large double bed. Beside the bed is a night table and a burning candle in a candlestick. A door opens and a horse playing the part of an out-of-town visitor enters. It approaches the table on its hind legs and takes a seat, crossing its knees. The horse rings a bell and immediately another horse appears. This is the "waitress" in a white apron and cap, who brings in his dinner. The visitor eats, sends the waitress off with the dirty dishes and then lies down on the bed. It pulls up the sheet, then the blanket, blows out the candle and "goes to sleep." The horses have been excellently trained and go through the entire script without prompting from their trainer.

Korolyov presents a very different type of training. At the beginning of his act the circus lights go out. plunging the circus in darkness. Then a narrow strip of light is beamed on a beautiful scene: a motionless white Arabian steed is posed with several persons grouped around it. We take in the sculptured group and once again the circus is plunged in darkness. This time the spotlight reveals a new "sculptural group." Here we see the work of an experienced trainer and artist.

The sound of oriental music heralds the next act. The great circular curtain raises on a tropical scene of a small lake, palm trees and cliffs. Musk ducks are perched on the shore of the lake. Cranes, storks and peacocks wander among the rocks. bamboo trees and cacti. Then the trainer appears and miracles begin to happen. He casts in his line and pulls out a crocodile! The little hillock he is sitting on turns into a live hippopotamus, an antilope leaps over it while a huge boa-constrictor winds itself about the trainer, hissing loudly.

Stepan Isaakyan, the trainer, had never had any previous experience before he began rehearsing this act with a·mixed group of exotic animals and birds. He had come to the circus with a burning desire to be a trainer. His persistence, willpower, ability and the help of experienced trainers made his dream come true. In 1958, circus audiences witnessed what they had always considered to be zoo animals performing in a circus.

Trained animals appear in many films, as was the case with the group of lions I was working with at the time.

Potap, a bear trained by Ivan Ruban, appeared in *The Last Act*. A lion from the Leningrad Zoo, born and bred in captivity, took part in *Don Quixote, She Loves You*, and *The New Adventures of Puss-in-Boots*. The lion actor Vasilyok was no longer a wild beast, he was competent in the role he had been assigned. Vasilyok has a truly rare character. He has appeared in three films and has won the love and admiration of all his colleagues. He was always anxious for his trainer to give him a gentle pat or tug.

Dangerous Paths and *The Tiger-Tamer* called for a group of trained tigers. As there was no such group, the "actors" had to be chosen from among several wild young Ussuri tigers. A Bengal tiger named Pursh was borrowed from the Riga Zoo to play the only role which had a tiger in close contact with one of the actresses. Pursh's gentle nature made it possible for us to train him for the film. A young woman who had previously been a variety show performer was taken on as the leading lady's

Furs are becoming to any woman,

but live furs are Elvira Podchernikova's speciality

which makes men a bit wary of her

stand-in for scenes where she was to appear with the tigers. When the filming was over the young lady, whose name was Margarita Nazarova, said she would like to remain with the group of tigers and become a professional trainer. I spent the next several months teaching her the ins and outs. When her act was ready and she was prepared to appear alone, she entered the brightly-lit circus ring. Today, Margarita Nazarova and her striped beauties are known throughout the country and abroad.

Max Borisov was a heavy-set man of medium stature with fierce, glittering eyes. In the ring he wore a plaid shirt and jeans and carried a great many revolvers to stress the fact that he was surrounded by vicious lions. He toured many cities of Russia, giving hundreds of performances. As the years passed his son grew up and, according to circus tradition, he followed in his father's footsteps. Vladimir Borisov became a lion-tamer. Though he had inherited his father's profession he did not inherit his methods or style of work, which were steeped in the traditions of the old school.

Vladimir Borisov is not yet thirty. He performs with a group of eight tremendous lions, all of whom he has personally trained. His father never knew the success his son has achieved, for he considered strength and terror the only means of training animals, while the younger Borisov is an advocate of the Soviet school of animal-training.

Ivan Kudryavtsev made his circus debut with his bear Gosha several years ago. Kudryavtsev leads Gosha into the ring and steps aside, leaving the stage to his pupil. Gosha, who weighs 200 kilos, rides a scooter, does somersaults and a handstand on parallel bars, and, finally, plays leap-frog with his teacher. In all, the bear does more than fifteen solo tricks. In conclusion, he embraces Kudryavtsev and makes him take a bow, as if to say, "Here's the man who taught me all I know."

Gosha's achievements are undoubtedly the result of patient training. Ivan Kudryavtsev was a collective-farm worker who saw his first circus performance in 1951, when he was nineteen. The last thing in the world he could have thought of then was that he would one day become an animal-trainer, for he had come to the city to enrol in an agricultural school. However, his first visit to the circus had such an effect on him that without a moment's hesitation he applied for a job as a bear-keeper, to help Sidorkina, a woman animal-trainer. In time, as he travelled about the country with the circus, Kudryavtsev acquired that which he wished for most desperately. It was a tiny bear cub, caught by hunters in Siberia. Kudryavtsev named him Gosha. He spent his days and nights with the bear until, finally, the door to success opened before him.

The script of *My Shaggy Friend* was written especially for Gosha and is a very popular comedy. Kudryavtsev recently took on a second pupil, a little bear cub named Shmelyok, who is being trained as Gosha's clowning assistant.

In speaking of animal-trainers, one can never forget the people who do so much for the success of so many acts. These are the trainer's assistants. For some strange reason no one ever speaks of them, yet it is mostly due to their efforts that the large animal acts come off so smoothly. The trainer maps out the act and sets the pace, with an experienced assistant as his right-hand man. He does all the dirty work, all the preparatory backstage work. This dangerous work with animals brings people very close together, and often it is unnecessary for the trainer to instruct his assistants during rehearsals or performances. Just as a surgeon's assistant understands him at a glance during a major operation, here, too, the assistant understands the trainer and knows what is expected of him at any given moment. This mutual understanding simplifies their work and brings rehearsals to a sooner completion.

In the past few years there has been a noticeable vogue in wild animal acts, for this effective performance attracts many. Sometimes established performers leave their acts to start a new career, that of training animals. Many young newcomers have chosen this field and are taught by experienced trainers.

The training of wild animals is the most difficult and dangerous type of circus work. It has a constant halo of adventure about it. The trainer's life is very interesting but it is fraught with danger whenever he is with his animals. That is why he must have extraordinary will-power and courage.

There is no place for hacks in the field of animal-training. Our audiences want to see a well-produced, beautiful performance of unusual animals. The skill of the trainers, those marvellous actors in the ring and selfless workers backstage, is always a cause for admiration and respect.

The trainer must also be a teacher, a doctor and a psychologist. Why is this animal feeling bad today? Why doesn't it have a good appetite? Why has a gentle and obedient animal hidden away in a corner of its cage, no longer responding to the kind words of its trainer? He can and must know all the answers. All day long the trainer is busy with his animals. Often, he spends the night with them as well, and such a schedule leaves very little time for his own personal life.

In my long years in the circus I have been clawed many times by wild animals, they have left many scars, but each and every time such a thing happened, it would be stored away in my memory as an unpleasant incident; my love for the circus and for my profession have always taken the upper hand.

An animal always senses the trainer's concern for it and his attitude towards it and even the trainer's mood when he comes to work. In each group of animals I worked with there were always those that were especially attached to me.

In 1940, I trained a group of seven large polar bears and toured with them for several years. When I decided to put on a new act, I handed my polar bears over to another trainer. One of the seven was a big bear named Mira. I usually appeared together with my wife Tamara. Nina and Mikhail Elvorti were aerialists who had become animal-trainers. They were to take over my bears.

I am always cautious about introducing new people to my animals. At first, Mikhail entered the cage between my wife and me. After a while, he became used to the animals and worked with them under my watchful eye. When the bears finally accepted him I left the cage. My wife continued to work with him. Soon Nina was introduced in the same manner. Now both Mikhail and Nina were working with the bears, while my wife remained in the cage "just in case."

Everything seemed to be going along smoothly. "This will be the last day Tamara stays in the cage. They can manage quite nicely without her," I decided one day. When rehearsals began I took a seat in the third row. This was a decisive day, for the group was soon to leave for Yaroslavl.

The performance was to begin with a mock wrestling match between a bear and a man. Mira always liked this game and would wave his paws about excitedly, squint and shake his head, trying to keep his "opponent" from grabbing him by the neck. After the wrestling match he and another bear would hitch themselves into a sledge and pull me off backstage.

But this time Mira rose up on his hind legs lazily and then, turning his head to one side, he headed towards Elvorti, coming down suddenly on all fours and lumbering off to the sledge. The second bear was confused, it hopped from foot to foot. After all, there should have been a wrestling match. But since there hadn't been any, what was he to do? And so he remained where he was.

"What's the matter?" I shouted and headed quickly towards the cage.

As I ran down the rows I saw Mira rise up on his hind legs. Sniffing loudly, he headed for the sound of my voice. He had not seen me for over a month. When I ran into the cage I was greeted by the mighty and happy roar of a colossal bear standing full height on his hind legs. Stretching his nose towards me and wobbling comically he extended his front paws and headed in my direction, as if inviting me to wrestle. This was against all the rules. The bear had to obey his new trainers.

"Tamara, don't let him come towards me!" I said to my wife. She stood in front of me and raised her baton. The bear looked down his nose at her, put one paw on her shoulder and "gently," but insistently pushed her aside. Mira was not as gentle with Mikhail and kicked him, sending him sprawling on the props. Thus he got rid of the "interference" and continued happily towards me. I could not resist such a show of affection. Mira embraced me and growled contentedly. It was a touching scene. We had to end the rehearsal then and there.

My story of these animals and my encounters with them might seem strange when I speak of them as sensible creatures, but many were the times when their behaviour, their attachment for me and the lasting effect of acquired instinct were really surprising.

These are but a few incidents in a life full of fascinating memories. I would like to wish the young people now taking up our difficult profession the best of luck and success. I have great faith in them.

In the many years of the Soviet circus our trainers have achieved much, but their greatest achievement of all is the creation of a Soviet school of animal-training.

1961

THE BIG RING

(Excerpt from the book
"Margarita Nazarova")

By M. Lobodin

Margarita Nazarova did not immediately discover her true calling in life. There were many sharp turns on the road, one of which was a stretch in the operetta and her interest in dancing.

It seemed at the time that this was where she would make her mark. But this was deceiving. Her passionate love for animals eventually made her choose animal-training as her career, though it was certainly a difficult and most dangerous one.

It was a happy day, indeed, when the circus management told her she would be taken on as a tiger-trainer, to work with the animals she had already appeared with in two films. Once again Boris Eder took on the double task of training his pupil and the tigers. He was teaching the animals to perform in a caged-in ring surrounded by large crowds.

Margarita was a dedicated pupil. They rehearsed doggedly for three straight months. Then she spent many hours with her four tigers in the ring of the Kostroma Circus, appearing before an imaginary audience, until her teacher finally decided the act was ready and Margarita could go on alone.

For a behind-the-scenes glimpse, let us look in on a rehearsal at the Kostroma Circus.

A stout iron cage surrounded the ring, with an iron tunnel made of heavy fencing leading into it. In the ring were Eder, Konstantinovsky, Nazarova and four tigers.

Margarita was working with the animals. She made them jump over obstacles, through a paper hoop and a flaming iron hoop.

Pursh, growling fondly, obeyed her command. He jumped onto a pedestal, gingerly tried out the narrow plank that lay between it and another pedestal, and then walked carefully across it. Nazarova wanted him to do it again, and Pursh gladly repeated the trick. The other three, Rada, Baikalochka and Achilles, followed suit. The trick was repeated over and over, and over again, to achieve perfect ease.

The "merry-go-round" trick was more difficult, and the animals did not always obey Margarita. They seemed to be annoyed at something. Suddenly Achilles snapped at Rada. The tigress howled, roared and smacked Achilles on the muzzle.

113

Margarita laughed at them and restored order sternly, sending them back to their places and returning to the small platform in the middle of the ring.

"Let's go!" she said, raising her little stick. Pursh rose up on his hind legs. The orchestra began to play, and the tiger began pushing a little merry-go-round, gaining speed every second.

The tigers were excited by the movement, as was Nazarova herself. She tapped her foot to the music and steered their performance in low tones.

Boris Eder watched his pupil's manner in the ring.

From time to time he offered a suggestion, sometimes he would take her place to demonstrate a fine point. This is how the act called "Trained Tigers" was readied for the audience.

"Nazarova is undoubtedly talented," the performers of the Kostroma Circus agreed. "She has the courage, the desire and the spirit to succeed that are so necessary to a true circus performer!"

Margarita worked hard at improving her style. Her teacher suggested that she show the audience things they never expected to see. Everyone knows that animals are afraid of fire; fire is man's best protection against wild beasts. All the more reason why the idea of sending tigers through a flaming hoop was so enticing. How could this be done? How could the animals be taught to accept fire? It all turned out to be much simpler than it seemed.

Nearly a year before the act was ready the trainers began rehearsing the tigers to jump through a flaming hoop. At first, they taught them to jump over a wire bent into an arc. Every time the tiger jumped over it, it was given a piece of meat as a reward. And this was repeated an endless number of times.

Meanwhile, the two ends of the arc were being brought closer and closer together, until they were finally joined to form a hoop. However, this was a very unusual sort of hoop with electric bulbs mounted all around it. As soon as the tigers could sail smoothly through the hoop, the trainers began getting them used to fire. This was the most difficult stage of the act. But here again the tasty tidbit awaiting the tiger at the

114

The great jungle beast flies through the air with the greatest of ease

What a warm rug for a cold winter's day!

other side of the hoop, the gentle voice and caress of the trainer, bolstered its desire to do its part.

Three or four electric lights would be turned on in the rim of the hoop. The tiger would look at it suspiciously, but there, standing beyond the lights, was Margarita with a piece of meat, calling to the animal gently: "Here! Come here!"

The temptation was too great, and the tiger would overcome its instinctive hatred of fire to jump through the hoop and receive its piece of meat, while Margarita stroked its ears fondly or patted its back. Each time a few more lights were put on in the hoop, but the animal was now used to them and paid no attention, since they were no longer a cause for worry.

Then the electric lights were replaced by tiny torches with real fire. First two, then four, then six. Finally, the entire hoop was a mass of fluttering flames. But the greedy tigers kept on jumping through the hoop in their quest for the piece of meat and the gentle words of their trainer on the other side. Thus, they forgot about the fire and their inborn fear of it. Practice had taught them that fire was not such a dangerous obstacle if only they took it at a single jump. Once the jump was completed, a reward awaited them.

When the hoop finally became a mass of fire, and hissing flames rose up threateningly from it, the tigers boldly jumped through it at a signal from their trainer. Then, after nearly ten months and 250 rehearsals, the act was ready.

On February 23, 1955, Margarita Nazarova made her debut as an animal-trainer, appearing with a group of tigers. The floor of the ring was covered with sawdust. A paper hoop was set up on a high stand at the entrance to the ring. The picture on the hoop was of a cat's head with a large blue bow tied around its neck. A blue-eyed young woman dressed in a black velvet suit trimmed with white silk walked over to the hoop. Her only weapon was a very small whip.

The audience received her with a due amount of distrust. Then she issued her first command. There was a roll of drums, the sound of paper tearing and a tiger's huge body flashed into the ring, landing softly on the sawdust.

"It's a tiger!" an excited whisper went through the audience.

Thus, Pursh, a Bengal tiger, made his own circus debut. He walked slowly over to a leather sofa and perched upon it, making the audience laugh. Margarita sat down next to him and began patting the fierce animal and scratching his ears.

Just then three other tigers appeared and trotted to their places. A branching oak stood in the centre of the ring. Margarita said something to the animals and began climbing quickly. The tigress did not wait to be spoken to again. In a leap and a bound she was beside the tree and began climbing the trunk, jumping from branch to branch, trying to catch up with the woman.

A comedy entitled *The Tiger-Trainer* was playing in many cinemas of the Soviet Union at the time. It was also shown to a group of French film representatives. As soon as the lights went on after the showing the Frenchmen wanted to know how the trick scenes were shot, for the impression was really one of a woman inside a cage of tigers.

They did not believe that there were actually very few trick shots in the picture, nor, certainly, that the trainer, Margarita Nazarova, whom they had just seen in the film could also be seen any evening at the Kostroma Circus.

"We will never believe you had a woman in a cage with Ussuri tigers," they said.

The doubting clients requested that a cameraman be sent to Kostroma to film either a rehearsal or a performance of the courageous trainer. The shots he brought back finally convinced them, and they were unanimous in bidding for the film.

* * *

Each day in the circus brought something new, but best of all was the actual show. The trainers always prepared for it as for a festive event, they sought to increase their ties with the audience. Millions of Soviet people were interested in art and culture, there were millions of circus fans in the country, and the old building, with a seating capacity of 2,000 was obviously too small. Circus performers dreamt of a "big ring" where hundreds of thousands of people, no, millions of people, would be able to see the performances. Soon, they found what they had been looking for. The tiger-trainers were invited to take part in a new comedy *The Striped Journey*, to be produced by Leningrad Film Studio, with tigers playing the leads. The

118

Work and play go hand in hand

script called for a dozen of tigers, a lion, a monkey and a very ordinary grey mouse.

It was a fascinating offer, for so much more could be done in a film than in the 13-metre circus arena. Now the animals could be shown in their various moods: playful and mean, complacent and wild, swimming and jumping. The main thing was to see that the script was not binding, that it gave the animals every opportunity to act naturally, even in the most unusual surroundings.

Soon V. Konetsky, a young sailor-turned-writer, and A. Kapler, a screen writer, had the script of a fine comedy ready for production. Margarita Nazarova was to play one of the leads, while her husband and assistant, Konstantinovsky, would get the animals ready. The opening scene showed a Soviet freighter, sailing across the Indian Ocean, bound from Ceylon to the U.S.S.R. with a cargo of tigers and lions. Suddenly, the animals managed to escape from their cages while the ship was in the middle of the raging ocean. Some evil hand had opened the cages. The crew scattered in panic, leaving the ship unattended, while the sailors tried desperately to get the animals back into their cages. Everyone took part in the struggle, the seamen, the navigator, the first mate, the cook, the waitress Mariana and the captain. But the animals fought for their newly found freedom, granted them by the mischievous monkey Pirate.

How could the film have been shot, with tigers and lions roaming in close proximity to people on the narrow decks? The shooting was done in the small area between the bow and stern, on the bridge, on deck, in the wheel-house and crew's quarters.

This was no easy task for the trainers, as their usual methods could not apply in such conditions. They had to think of something new, of something that would make it possible for the actors to perform without fear of the animals and for the animals to appear perfectly natural in the film.

V. Fetin, the producer, said the animals should feel as much at home on shipboard as they would in the jungle, for then, and then only, would the film ring true.

Konstantinovsky began working on the script, and, as could have been expected, he soon became an assistant director—trainer.

120

Naturally, the script had to be based on action. It would have normally taken from ten months to a year to "teach" the wild animals to behave according to the story, but the deadline was set much closer than that.

How could the animals be made to act properly? Konstantinovsky decided not to make the tigers perform at all! He said they must take advantage of whatever the animals themselves "suggested." The tigers would thus improvise as they went along, while the director and cameraman would merely guide them. In this way the lion would behave as a true lion should in accordance with his acting "abilities," his age and his temperament as a "star."

Everything was set for rehearsals to begin on board a ship at sea. Konstantinovsky had been given two months instead of the ten or twelve months normally required. In these two months all the animals would have to complete a special course of training.

Work was begun. The old freighter *Matros Zheleznyak*, scheduled for the graveyard, was turned into a floating rehearsal hall by the staff of the Leningrad Studio. "Warning! Tigers Aboard!" read the big poster near the gangplank. Smaller posters with the same warning were hung about the ship. The freighter, with a new four-metre-high iron fence attached to the railing, was now given over to the tigers. The animals wandered up and down the decks, playing and cavorting, enjoying their sudden freedom.

The tigers could not stop when they wanted to on the slippery deck, and when they did, they bumped into doors and ladders, which then came crashing down. It was very difficult for the animals to become accustomed to their unusual surroundings. Margarita and Konstantinovsky "visited" them every day, to see how they were coming along, to discover what each was most interested in.

One of the tigers proved to be a lover of heights and was often seen climbing the masts, ladders and the narrow planks thrown between the roofs of the deck structures. They decided to use this in the film.

Once, when the tigers were climbing to the bridge, one of them balked at the narrow ladder. Konstantinovsky forced it into the first mate's cabin. The tiger made a dash for the porthole, knocking out the frame and window when it jumped through it to the deck. This was also to be included in the script.

Two tigresses were fascinated by the portholes. They sniffed at them and stuck their paws through the openings, trying to get at whatever it was on the other side. Kalva, a young and beautiful tigress, was especially fond of the bulwark. She would often stand there on her hind paws, leaning on it as she gazed dreamily at the waves below. Truly, an excellent scene.

Long before the actual shooting began, Konstantinovsky went to Kiev to "meet" one of the leading characters, a trained chimpanzee named Pirate. Their acquaintance began with a row, when Pirate attacked the strange man who had dared enter his cage without an invitation. Konstantinovsky covered his face with his hands and made-believe he was crying. Pirate stopped hitting him, put his arm around the "crying" man and began patting his head with his hairy hand. However, Pirate refused to leave his cage until his girl-friend, Chilita, was taken along. Thus, with their arms around each other fondly, they left Kiev for their "tour" of Leningrad.

They travelled by boat and were put in the wireless room. Half an hour later they felt quite at home there. Chilita behaved nicely, fussing around the canvas covers on the wireless apparatuses, but Pirate raced about the boat and soon knew every nook and cranny. He made a nuisance of himself, begging the sailors for candy and cigarettes, getting in everyone's way, grabbing at anyone who passed by, trying to scare them, stick-

Everyone goes on vacation together

ing out his tongue at them. After a while he climbed the mast and began doing tricks and showing off.

The crew took a liking to the chimp and presented him with a regulation striped sweatshirt. Pirate was in ecstasy. He put on the shirt himself, grabbed a mop from an unwary sailor and began swabbing down the deck. The sailors roared with laughter, while the trainer jotted the incident down in his little book for further use. There were many scenes in the film where Pirate was left to himself and did the most unexpected things. This made the role of the actor who appeared in the same scenes with him rather difficult, as he had to play along by ear within the general framework of the scene.

The lion Vasya did not present as difficult a problem, for he was an old hand at films, having appeared in *Don Quixote*, *She Loves You* and *The New Adventures of Puss-in-Boots*. Kalva, Vektorsha and Loyda were the only tigers who had never appeared in films before, and now they followed their leader Ural diligently.

At first, Vasya was wary of Margarita, but he could not hold out long in the face of her gentle words, and soon they were fast friends. According to all indications, he was "getting ready" for his new part. Since he was an old trouper, he "understood" what "preparatory work" meant. Margarita rehearsed with him every day, she sat on his back, pulled his tail, threw him to the ground and did everything the script called for.

Meanwhile, the tigers were going through their paces nicely. In the film Margarita was to play the captain's niece, the ship's waitress Mariana, and she tried to make the animals act in accordance with the script.

Despite her heavy schedule in the circus she used every spare moment for studying the art of acting. She was accepted as an "observer" at the Actor's Studio of the well-known film director, Sergei Gerasimov. There she attended lectures and received training in a group headed by Tamara Makarova, film actress and pedagogue.

Shooting began with the last episode of the film. It showed Mariana, now a veterinary surgeon, taking a sick tiger to an animal hospital in an open car. Pursh's bandaged muzzle looked very comical. Mariana was comforting her unhappy patient, pressing its head to her. Thus they rode through the main streets of Leningrad, followed by the surprised and worried stares of passers-by. Pursh behaved beautifully. He sat in the car as if he understood that he was being photographed and must play his part and paid no attention to the people in the streets.

The first day of filming was a success. The next day they were to move to the ship. They had a tight schedule, for the short Leningrad summer was ending. All the ocean scenes were to be taken in the Black Sea near Odessa. But then everything had to be put off to welcome Margarita's new son, Alexei, into the world.

Soon, however, they went on location to the Black Sea Coast. Instead of the old reliable *Matros Zheleznyak* they had used for rehearsals they were given another freighter, the *Fryazino*. The filming was done in the sea between Odessa and Batumi. At times the crew became actors, as when, according to the script, the ship was taken over by wild beasts. A second ship was used during the really dangerous scenes when everyone not actually taking part in them was transferred to it. The cameraman and electrician and their equipment were entrenched in specially-built cages, for there were tigers roaming everywhere!

Not everything came off smoothly, however. There were mistakes, but they were corrected along the way. The trainers often discussed them while relaxing in the messroom.

One of the mishaps occurred near Odessa at the very end of the filming. The tigers were roaming about on the bow, and

Kalva was behaving strangely. She would go up to the bulwark and gaze down at the waves, then walk away, only to return again. She did this several times. Before the trainers realised what she was up to, the tigress had jumped overboard.

Kalva was now swimming away from the ship. The trainers were not afraid she would drown, but they were afraid she might come upon one of the many small boats. Tragedy certainly awaited its occupants. More terrifying yet was the possibility that she might swim ashore and come up on the crowded beach among strangers.

The captain stopped the ship as a motor launch was lowered over the side. The trainers got in and set out in search of Kalva, but no matter how carefully they scrutinised the area, they could find no trace of her, and were finally forced to return to the ship. While they were out searching, another incident took place aboard ship. When the first mate heard the sound of the motor launch he ran up on

Travelling fosters lasting friendships

deck, not knowing that some of the animals were still out of their cages. He discovered this a bit late, when he came face to face with Vektorsha, a young tigress.

He sprang back and raced up to the top deck with the tiger hot on his heels and growling fiercely. He then sailed through the air in a record leap which, unfortunately, was child's play for Vektorsha, and finally managed to escape, leaving a large piece of his tunic in her teeth. The tigress was led off, but she was sullen as she entered her cage, having been stopped in the middle of such an interesting hunt.

Nearly an hour had passed from the time the alarm had first been sounded. The minutes dragged on. However, everything ended as unexpectedly as it had begun when Kalva's head suddenly appeared in the water near the ship. She had had her fun, felt nice and refreshed, and now wanted to come back again. Her wish was quickly granted. Glancing neither to right nor to left, she trotted guiltily to

And one gains valuable experience that comes in handy later

her cage. From then on, though she still gazed longingly at the bulwark and the cool waves of the sea, her trainers watched her closely, never giving her a chance to repeat her performance.

At times incidents occurred that were neither mistakes nor misjudgements, but which proved very upsetting. Thus, we were shooting a scene about 100 yards offshore in which the tigers were to try and save the waitress Mariana who had fallen overboard. They were to swim with her towards the shore.

Five tigers were placed in a large cage which was then attached to a crane. At a signal from the cameraman, the crane operator began lowering the cage of tigers into the water. Everyone expected the animals to crawl out through the open cage door and swim after Margarita, while the assistant cameraman, who was perched on top of the cage, shot the scene from above.

At first everything went according to plan. The cage was slowly lowered into the water. Margarita swam about nearby. Seeing the door of their cage open, the tigers made their way out. First one, then another, then a third began swimming after Margarita. But the fourth, Ural, the most powerful and fiercest of them all, did not want to be forced into a cold bath. He scrambled to the top of the cage and sat down next to the assistant cameraman and his helpers. He was soon followed by the fifth and last tiger who shook the water off himself angrily.

The men on top of the cage were petrified. Coming to their senses, they jumped into the sea, clothes and all, and swam after Margarita and the other three tigers. Ural, the conquerer, watched them paddle away.

Of the ten tigers in Margarita Nazarova's group seven are excellent swimmers. This is a most unusual feat. About twenty years ago Bendix, a famous trainer, said that a tiger could be taught to jump through burning hoops but it could never be made to get into the water. Contrary to his opinion, Soviet

128

trainers see to it that all their young tigers learn to swim, dive and play in the water.

There is much to be said of the film *The Striped Journey* and of the work of the trainers that went into it. After seeing the picture in Moscow, a Hollywood film-maker said that he and his colleagues were amazed at the part the tigers played in the film and at the unusual way in which these wild beasts were presented. Until then it had been an established fact that any film with such large, ferocious animals ended in tragedy. But the Soviet script-writers, producers, trainers and actors found this tradition unacceptable. Now, for the first time, audiences could see a lively comedy in which tigers played the leads. He went on to say that though he did not know Russian, he had laughed throughout the film, for one did not have to know the language to understand it. Tigers in a comedy were really something unheard-of.

* * *

Anyone who loves the circus and is used to seeing strength, courage, skill and physical beauty triumph in the ring cannot but admire Margarita Nazarova, the trainer of fierce wild beasts. Though she does not boast great physical strength, the power of her will, the will of a person who subdues wild beasts, is apparent to all.

Though Margarita Nazarova is an unusual woman, she is not unique. Her talent is but another link in the chain of such great talents as Eder, Gladilshchikov, Bugrimova, Ruban and Kudryavtsev.

From the very start of her circus career she was fortunate to have had the best teachers, famous masters in their field, the concern and attention of her colleagues, and the general atmosphere of friendship and good-will that reign in the Soviet circus.

1962

WALTER
ZAPASHNY'S
DUEL

By L. Adov

Walter Zapashny is a very modest man. When asked about himself, he prefers to discuss the animals he works with. These include lions and tigers, panthers and a mean and nervous lynx. Not many of the other animals are mild-mannered either. Walter never uses the word "beast" when speaking of them, for he does not like the word. And truly, though they are not always obedient, to him they are not beasts, they are his charges, he has brought them up and educated them in a long and difficult struggle.

His appearances at the Moscow Circus can without exaggeration be called triumphant. The Soviet circus has never known anything like his act, though we have seen many animal-trainers, both at home and abroad. Walter Zapashny's first performances in Moscow were a landmark in circus history.

There is nothing menacing and nothing gaudy in his appearance. He does not come on as a god in glittering breeches or in a tunic adorned with pompous shoulder-straps, nor does he have a billowing red-lined cape thrown carelessly over his shoulder. He does not appear bare-chested to amaze the audience with his grand physique. One should note, however, that Walter is a Master of Sports in gymnastics, acrobatics

Walter Zapashny is a modern D'Artagnan

whose words are promptly heeded

Getting angry won't help

nor will running away

When Walter gets down on his knee,
his animals follow suit

and a good laugh ends it all

and weight-lifting. He does not instil fear in his animals by cracking a whip, and if he occasionally does fire blank cartridges into the air they are merely a token of the old tradition, and even the animals cast an ironic glance at him when he does. They are not at all afraid of him, for who was ever afraid of a friend! In fact, they seem to love him and to respect him for being just. If he does punish one of them, there is good reason why he has done so.

Walter is both demanding and strict and will not put up with familiarity. If an animal does its work well, it receives its reward, if it doesn't it has no one to blame but itself and goes off to a corner. And the lions and tigers, the panthers and the lynx all give in to man's will. See how obedient they are! What discipline, how well they perform. Walter rides into the ring on a lion. One feels that though the lion is obedient, it is by no means oppressed. In fact, it seems proud to be carrying such a strong, courageous man on its back. Following the entrance of the king of the beasts, the tigers and panthers go through a series of jumps, leaping high over each other. A tigress walks between the trainer's legs just like a lap-dog. The evil-looking lynx does not have to be prompted to

When you're starting out, someone has to take the lead

And you'll need a drummer

There are obstacles to be overcome on the way

run over to the drum and beat it. The tigers stretch out side by side on the floor, pressing close together, forming a magnificent striped carpet. The animals leave the ring just as effectively, jumping through a high glittering hoop.

There is a very sly ending to the act. Typhoon, a real wit, is the last to leave, and he nonchalantly flips the catch on the door as he exits.

These difficult tricks demand that the actions of several wild animals be co-ordinated and synchronised, and that the whole have an air of ease and grace. No one knows how difficult it was for the trainer to achieve this or how he won the right to stand with his back turned to these man-eaters! Not many have done this before, and no one has ever worked with a group of tigers of different species. Zapashny has a Bengal, an Indian and an Ussuri tiger. As if this were not enough, he has taught them to keep their peace, working in a group with black Malayan panthers and a vicious South China lynx!

Walter Zapashny's friendship with these cats was born of struggle. He is right when he says that his work is a duel, that each day in the past six years that he has spent training his animals has been a duel, that each step he takes in the ring is a duel as well.

The very first encounter, during his debut in Ivanovo, ended in tragedy. Bagira, a tigress, took advantage of a moment when Walter had his back to her and attacked him. His presence of mind and strength saved him from imminent death as he grabbed the animal's head and pressed it so hard against the back of his own head that the tigress could not open her mouth. By the time his helpers managed to tear her away she had clawed his shoulders, back and legs. The act was cancelled and Walter was

rushed to a hospital, where he spent the next month and a half in bed.

After such a "debut" the acrobat-turned-animal-trainer might well have decided to take up his former profession again, for it was undoubtedly easier on the nerves. But Walter was not one to give in quickly. He returned to the ring and took up where he had left off with the same perseverance as before. The joy of success soon followed.

"Animals are amazingly observant," Walter said. "They are also very sensitive. It is not easy to discover what they are really like, but I'm convinced that the wildest one can also experience gratitude. I remember once Sultan became gravely ill. It looked like the end had come, but I stayed in his cage with him for three days and three nights, doing what I could to ease his pain. And he got well.

"I'll never forget the way Sultan looked at me the day the crisis had passed. It was a look full of gratitude and faith. That was three years ago, but Sultan has never forgotten, he has never stopped expressing his friendship for me."

One must see Bagira and Sultan performing in the ring to appreciate Walter Zapashny's

He doesn't care much for fruit juice

but a fellow-cat arouses his interest. However, the stranger seems to have a heart of stone

skill. The once fierce tigress now trots around on her hind legs for her master, obeying his every command. And Sultan the lion, the great king of the beasts, behaves like a kitten, rubbing his mane gently against his trainer's knees, gazing up at him devotedly. Such feelings cannot be taught. The animals are under the spell of Walter's charm, they have responded to his firm, kind hand.

And yet each day spent working with them is a duel, a duel in which man's mind and will-power have triumphed.

1964

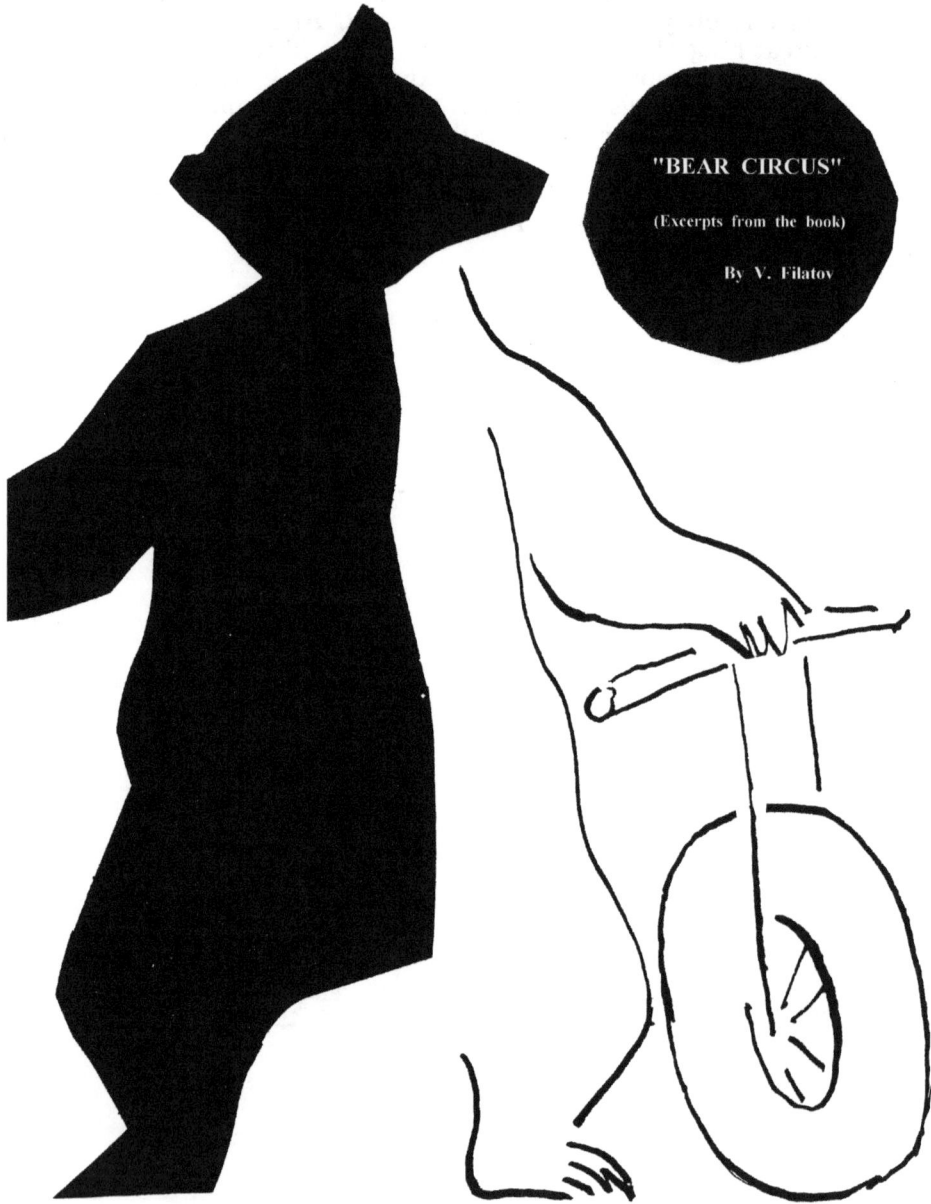

"BEAR CIRCUS"

(Excerpts from the book)

By V. Filatov

It was decided that we would fly to the Far East. My bears (there were 14 of them by then) had never travelled any other way than by railroad or truck. Naturally, I was a bit apprehensive of how they would behave in the air. To tell the truth, I was a bit worried myself, for I had never flown such a long distance by transport plane. Just before we boarded the plane we discovered that the bears' cages were too big. We had to leave them at the airport and take the bears on with nothing more than their muzzles, fastening their leashes to the inside walls of the plane.

The crew had gathered in a little group to a side and were laughing at the way I had to shove the balking bears into the plane. The flimsy ladder fell several times and both I and the bear on it would come tumbling down. The animals were nervous. The smell of gasoline and the roar of planes coming in and taking off irritated and frightened them.

When all my passengers were finally settled, the crew followed us in. Now it was my turn to laugh, for they pressed close to the opposite wall as they inched towards the cockpit.

There was the deafening roar of motors warming up. The bears huddled together, shaking from fright. As soon as the plane took off they all toppled to the floor. It was funny to see the way they covered their eyes with their

He doesn't care much for fruit juice

but a fellow-cat arouses his interest. However, the stranger seems to have a heart of stone

You can hear the driver's song across the steppe

paws. I made my way to the centre of the group and sat down among them. They moved over eagerly and gladly took me in, pressing close to me, seeking protection, and never once guessing that I was just as scared as they were. Thus huddled together we reached Khabarovsk.

It was difficult to rehearse in the circuses of Khabarovsk, Ussuriisk and Vladivostok. There were many acts on the bill and the ring was never vacant: several acts would always be rehearsing simultaneously, jugglers and acrobats, trapeze artists and rope-walkers. There was not enough room, but there was no way out, and so, the more the merrier! Those who really had no place to rehearse in the ring, rehearsed between the rows and aisles and in the corridors.

It was my lot to rehearse at night, though I managed to squeeze in a few hours in the daytime as well, rehearsing my bear circus in the yard, in the corridors, in a barn, in a stable and once even in the manager's waiting room! This was probably the hardest time of all. Most of my bears were approaching adolescence, their characters were changing, they were becoming irritable and mean. At times I felt like giving up, there were moments when I lost all faith in the success of our act.

However, my colleagues would not let me despair, they tried to cheer me up as best they could. This was especially true of Karandash (Mikhail Rumyantsev). He often came to my rehearsals. He was interested in my plans and gave me many useful suggestions. One of the characters in the act was a clowning bear.

A whole barrel of honey. What a treat!
Every girl should study ballet even if it comes out this way

Mikhail Rumyantsev not only helped me to create a "bear Karandash" but let me use several of his own comic tricks.

Karandash is an excellent actor, a master clown. He explained the secret of how to put the cart together to the circus carpenter and showed me how to hitch the goose to it. He sketched a pattern for the bear's pants for the circus dressmaker, he even drew a picture of the hat and coloured dickey that went with the costume.

I would like to tell you of a funny incident which happened many years later, when Karandash and I met again on tour in Riga.

Karandash has a funny skit called "The Donkey Bicycle" that was described earlier in this book.

The donkey's name was Grishka, and for some reason or other my bear Burket took an instant dislike to him. Perhaps he recalled the time when he was still a little cub and was frightened by a mule in a stable, and from then on could never stand the sight of any of his relatives. Perhaps the donkey's braying annoyed him, or perhaps what he really wanted was a tasty chunk of donkey flesh. His motives were unknown to me. But one thing was perfectly clear: the bear wanted to get his paws on

In this corner we give you the featherweight champion of the forest

A quick word of advice from his trainer between rounds

Rules aren't everything, you know

Grishka and was constantly after the unfortunate animal.

Though I kept a careful eye on Burket, he once managed to disappear behind the curtain during a performance. I found the runaway in the stable. The donkey was braying so loudly one might have thought it was being eaten alive. And there was good reason for its fright. Burket had Grishka in his paws, holding him high over his head. It looked as if he was ready to throw him to the ground. Then I saw a dismembered donkey leg on the floor! I gasped. Had Burket chewed it off? But the donkey had all its four legs. That could only mean it was the "spare tyre" leg.

I heaved a sigh of relief, rushed over to Burket and made him put the donkey down. Grishka had only a bad scare and a few scratches to show for the encounter, but Burket got a few hard slaps for his mischief.

After we completed our tour of the Far East we were to go on to Kalinin for a final "polishing" I was all ready to set out when I received word that I was expected in Yuzhny Sakhalinsk.

There had never been a circus there before, but the people of the city and the soldiers of the garrison had built a circus on their own

The heavyweight title match

Throwing in the towel

The new champion

initiative. It was built according to all the rules, with a regular ring, stables and other premises.

Once again we were air-bound. This time my charges were bolder, they strolled up and down the plane. The instrument panel showed 3,000 metres above sea level, with nothing but mist beyond the windows. The Tatar Strait was ahead of us, and we were coming in for a landing. I began to swallow and yawn to keep my ears from getting plugged when, to my great surprise, I saw that my bears all had their mouths wide open and were swallowing saliva. I had been told to do this, but who had told them? Had they guessed it by themselves?

When we landed in Yuzhny Sakhalinsk I discovered that there had been no announcement of our coming performances. How could we tell the people that the "Bear Circus" had arrived?

I got out the bears' bicycles, roller skates and scooters and thus we entered the city. I led the procession in a jeep with several of the bears, while the others rolled along behind under their own steam. That evening every ticket was sold. The only ones who were displeased by our cavalcade were the teachers of the city's schools, for no one came to classes that day, all the children were out in the streets greeting us. Our nine performances were completely sold out.

What won't people think of next!

Times being what they are, you have to keep up with the others

Top form at last!

Then I received a telegram from Moscow: "Bring bear circus Moscow. Opening season. Première November sixth. Return immediately."

This really was a blow, for the new tricks were ready in general outline only, they had as yet to be merged into a complete act. The props, equipment and costumes had not yet arrived from Leningrad, and there was less than two weeks left till the opening night. Once again we boarded a plane.

We landed in Moscow on October 29th with only eight days at our disposal. Our things arrived from Leningrad on the 30th, and fittings, etc., began. We rehearsed at night. The dress rehearsal was held on the 5th of November, the very eve of our opening.

Much of what had originally been planned never materialised. In the course of our rehearsals some tricks had been changed, others had been discarded entirely.

Nevertheless, the bear act was ready on schedule, though by then hardly anyone believed it would be.

The audience and critics received it well, but the most flattering opinion was a short paragraph in a book entitled *Notes of an Old Clown,* by Ivan Radunsky, Merited Artiste of the R.S.F.S.R., one of the veterans of the Russian circus and the oldest living clown, the creator of "Bim-Bom," the famous clowning musician.

"Filatov's 'Bear Circus' is an unusually interesting act, extremely popular with children and adults alike. I, who have seen dozens and even hundreds of animal acts, can say with confidence that the circus has never seen anything like it in all its history."

It took many months and even years to prepare and rehearse some of the tricks. For instance, I got the idea for a trick which had bears riding motorcycles in 1945, but was not able to present it until 1950. To tell the truth, no one at the Main Office believed it could be done. In 1949, I bought a Moskva motorcycle and began rehearsing with the bears on the quiet. I had to go down the entire list of my performers, for the noise of the motor, the clatter and the smell of gasoline frightened them. They became nervous at the very sight of the motorcycle.

I tried to teach the bears to get used to it by moving the cages into a circle in the stable, rolling the motorcycle into the middle and starting the motor.

145

A brave bear was found in their midst at last. His name was Taimur, and he then was my choice. I began rehearsing by giving him his food next to the clattering motorcycle. He would look at it angrily but kept on eating. Several days later I put Taimur on the seat, stuffing him with lumps of sugar all the while. A week later Taimur was calmly eating sugar while seated on the shaking, roaring motorcycle. It was not too comfortable a seat, for there was no place for his paws. That is why I removed the seat and replaced it with a broad board which I attached by means of a wire. Now Taimur was comfortable and he had a place to rest his paws.

The next step was to roll him around, and after that I could turn on the motor. Taimur was an excellent cyclist. He was a good judge of distance and had a marvellous sense of balance. That is why it did not take him long to become accustomed to the motorcycle. We rehearsed every day. The motorcycling bear first appeared at the Riga Circus.

Once Taimur had learned the trick, I taught Mura and Dimka how to ride a motorcycle. In the finale of our act the three bears rode into the ring on three motorcycles. However, I soon had to exclude one, as in their mad desire to overtake each other the bears would often collide and break their motorcycles.

They learned to turn on the headlights when the circus lights were dimmed and to turn them off when the lights went on again. Taimur and Dimka even know how to step on the gas, though after several races I don't let them do it any more.

I was especially proud of my riders when I came upon a photograph in a 1950 magazine of an animal-trainer and his motorcycle-riding bear. The bear was seated on a specially-designed motorcycle, with a special steering wheel, a special seat and special gears. My bears ride ordinary motorcycles without any special contraptions.

In Sverdlovsk I had a very bad accident during Murat's debute as a motorcycle rider. Murat is a huge, calm animal. He was quick in learning how to ride but was apparently stunned by the bright lights, loud music and applause as he rode out. He jumped right off the motorcycle and it fell with a bang. Murat became frightened and raced backstage, to the stable. I ran after him. I caught him near the curtain and pulled him back into the ring, but Murat pulled me backstage. We began wrestling. Suddenly Murat got his teeth and claws into my leg.

146

The best pupils put on a show

With great difficulty I managed to push him aside, but he lurched towards me again and his paws came crashing down on my shoulder with tremendous force. I thought something cracked in my spine but was too excited to pay attention to it.

I pushed his paws aside and felled him. Then, grabbing his collar, I dragged him to a post that was cemented in the floor and tied him to it securely. I wanted to return to the

These fellows have been at it longer

ring but could not, for my legs seemed to have turned to water. I became frightened and sank down to the floor next to the bear.

Ivan Anisimov, my assistant, came running over.

"What's wrong? What happened?" he shouted.

"I don't know. Go back and finish the act without me."

"But you need help."

"Go on back! I'll be right up."

Anisimov ran back into the ring. I tried to rise, but fell to the floor again. Several attendants carried me into the manager's office. Several moments later Anisimov came running in again.

"What a mess!"

"Now what's wrong?"

"This takes the cake! Taimur doesn't want to exit. He's done about twenty circles round the ring already. What shall I do?"

"Try to grab the seat from behind and head him towards the exit."

It was not easy to catch Taimur. He zigzagged this way and that to escape his pursuer. The audience enjoyed the chase immensely. Finally, Taimur was caught and the act was brought to a belated end.

My back was strapped and rehearsals continued as usual.

And what about Murat? His attitude did not change. Though he felt no special love for me, there was no special dislike, either. He treated me as he always had and probably forgot all about the incident. He eventually became an excellent rider.

I wanted to experiment, to find new tricks for my "Bear Circus." One can only develop as a performer if one constantly strives to improve. No matter if many well-rehearsed tricks are not included in the final version of the act, they have served their purpose, they have helped to awaken the imagination and increase your skill. That is why I can never agree with performers who, having once put an act together, appear with it till the end of their lives, never changing or improving it.

I now decided to create an act with a mixed group of horses and bears. I handed in an outline to the head office, was given a horse and began rehearsals.

The floor where I rehearsed was 11 metres in diameter. The diameter of all circus rings in the Soviet Union is a standard 15 metres. That left two metres on each side to the railing, which was quite enough for the horse to move around in.

We don't want anyone getting run over here

"Bears on Horseback" was rehearsed and presented. It began with a bear leading a horse into the ring. The bear saluted and the horse kneeled. Then the bear mounted the horse and galloped around the ring standing upright on its hind legs. Several small obstacles were set up, the horse jumped over them and walked under specially built arcs. As it walked under each one the bear would climb over it and jump onto the horse's back again. Then it did a handstand on a little platform. In conclusion, the horse placed its forelegs on the edge of the ring and nodded, thus greeting the audience, while the bear did a knee-bend and saluted. The horse then backed onto the middle of the ring, the bear picked up the reins and led it out. This trick riding was not part of the "Bear Circus" for long, since it could very well go on as an independent act.

I believe my experiments in the air were of special interest. I made use of Herman Reznikov's aerial torpedo and later Boris Levandovsky's special apparatus. I then began rehearsing a rather complex and effective trick, a flight under the Big Top. There were two participants, my bear Malchik and a gymnast. The man and Malchik would both hang by their teeth as they were raised to the top of the circus. The torpedo would then begin to circle over the arena. During this act Malchik would do four difficult acrobatic tricks, tricks which not every aerialist could repeat.

My bears were constantly taught new tricks. They learned how to roller-skate, to ride bicycles and motorcycles.

There are many plans ahead!

1962

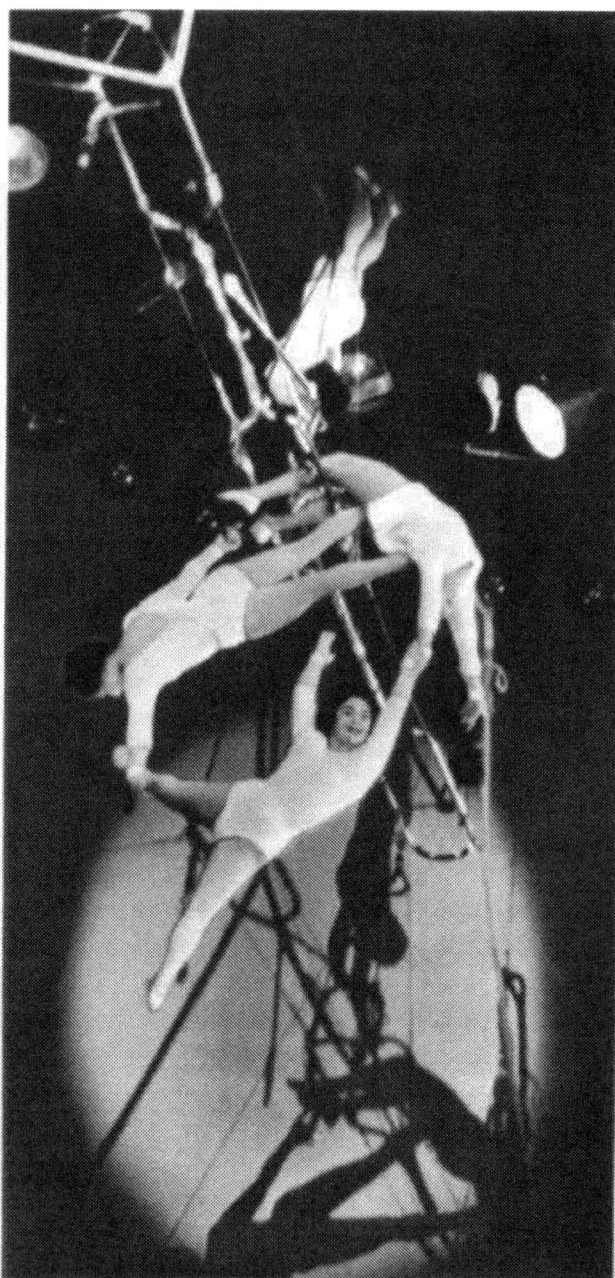

THE BLUE
DRAGON-FLIES
By M. Medvedev

When you see a playbill announcing the Bubnovs, the name that immediately comes to mind is "The Blue Dragon-Flies," as they were called in Paris and as the trapeze act has since been known.

From a professional point of view the act is produced and presented as follows. Three lightweight metal frames are connected by equally light bindings. This is the frail "stage" on which four pretty gymnasts perform on rings, and trapezes. There is precision in their movements, they change formation instantly and perform a series of most difficult and breath-taking tricks, all of which lead to the grand finale of the act, a dizzying aerial merry-go-round.

The Blue Dragon-flies make one wonder

whether they are really earthly creatures

Karandash decides they are ethereal

If we look at their act through the magic of a crystal ball we will certainly agree that the name they have fondly been given is a fitting one. The four young women are dressed in light-blue tights. They are illuminated from all sides as they flit about under the circus top, seemingly weightless, graceful and full of shimmering joy, bringing to mind fairy-tale dragon-flies. When they form a pyramid it seems as if they have become a single bright dragon-fly, hanging from a slender reed, glittering in the summer sun. Then the ring below ceases to be a circus ring and becomes a deep mysterious pond.

Backstage in their dressing-room after the act you find them very likable and charming.

A cursory glance will tell you that this dressing-room belongs to women, for only women can manage to have such a cosy and attractive confusion of costumes, the black, white, blue and green tights they use to change their "colouring."

The four gymnasts sit before a long dressing table, exchanging small-talk, laughing, fixing their hairdos and make-up, for they appear again in the grand finale.

There is an atmosphere of youth and good cheer in the room. The "dragon-flies" are very graceful and feminine, and the only telltale sign that these frail creatures are forever working with ropes and trapezes are the hard callouses on their hands, quite like the callouses of rowers.

We discover that the four Bubnovs are Yulia Ostrovinskaya, Tamara Akifyeva, Galina Perestoronina and Yelena Bubnova, the eldest of the four. The Bubnovs have been appearing for close to twenty years.

There have been many changes in the course of these years. There were other girls in the act who have left and new ones who have taken their places, but Yelena and Yulia are the two charter members who have carried on the act and its traditions. The reason why one or another of the girls would drop out was very understandable, for when a girl marries she wants to be with her husband. This was all but impossible if she worked in the circus, and so she eventually would leave the act. However, both Yelena and Yulia remained in the circus. Their act has become one of the best in the country and is famous abroad.

The four gymnasts have travelled far and wide in Europe, America, Africa and Cuba.

156

The following rather amusing incident took place in Cairo. The Soviet circus troupe was to leave Egypt for its scheduled performances in Yemen, when several representatives of the Yemeni circus arrived in Egypt.

"We cannot permit your performers to enter our country," they said.

"Why not?"

"Because they appear half-naked. And anyway, how can one permit women to fly through the air? Such a sight is not for the eyes of faithful Moslems."

Nevertheless, the puritanical representatives of Yemen were present at the evening performance. The moment the Bubnovs appeared they covered their faces with dark cloths. However, the cloths slipped lower and lower as the performance got under way, and when it was over and the four women slid down their ropes to the ground the men threw off the black cloths completely and applauded.

1963

THE VOLZHANSKYS

By V. Angarsky
and A. viktorov

Imagine a man crossing a tight-wire twenty metres over the ground. He is not alone; doing a one-handed handstand on his head is another man, and thus they proceed along the wire. Is this bravado? No, these are talented rope-walkers whose act is not based on a single hair-raising moment but on precise timing and great skill. Here is proof that average, well-trained men can conquer great heights and, relying on nothing save their strength and skill, make the impossible come true. Thus we are introduced to the Volzhanskys, "the mountain-climbers of the Moscow Circus," as they were called during their tour of Italy.

From the moment they appear in the ring to their final exit there is a charged atmosphere of awe and dread in the air.

The first tricks are jumps from a handstand on a platform high over the ring to a wheel raised to the same height, but placed a metre away from the platform; in other words, they are doing somersaults over a chasm. Next come jumps from a one-handed handstand position on a two-metre-high stilt. The performer had to rehearse the jump close to 100,000 times before it was perfect. These seemingly simple tricks succeed one another. Then from the middle of the ring, a revolving pedestal is raised to a height of twenty metres. Guy wires that look like rays lead from the pedestal to stationary platforms around the sides of the arena. The Volzhanskys, five in all, form a live pyramid on the pedestal. Then they move on to the wire. Vladimir Volzhansky carries Maria, who is doing a handstand on his head. Then he proceeds along the wire while she does a difficult acrobatic trick. The Volzhanskys are the first and only performers to have ever attempted this difficult trick. The pedestal rises higher still. The guy wires are now at a 45° angle to the platforms. Vladimir steps onto the wire from a side platform, carrying Nikolai Volzhansky in a handstand on his hands. Maria stands gracefully erect on one foot on Nikolai's

head. Can this be possible?! It seems unbelievable, for Vladimir is carrying his two partners up a wire at a 45° angle. When they reach the central pedestal he leaves his partners there. Now he takes up a two-wheeled roller-skate, does a one-handed handstand on it and slides down the wire to the ground. But he is carrying Maria, who is performing on a light trapeze attached to the roller-skate. This is truly phenomenal! These tricks lead up to the finale. A trampoline is set up on the inclined guy wire. Vladimir slides down the wire on a pair of two-wheeled roller-skates, gaining speed each moment. In no time he has reached the trampoline and in another moment he is flying through the air, coming down squarely on the wire again and sliding to the ground. This seems to embody Vladimir Volzhansky's courage, his years of experience and the road he has traversed.

Vladimir Volzhansky, leader of the troupe, has been a circus performer for twenty-five years. During this time he has created many original acts, performing tricks that seemed truly impossible. His performances are known for their artistry, choreography and drama. Until quite recently the troupe presented "Forest Fantasy" which included rope-walking, acrobatics and pyramids. It was a short fairy-tale pantomime in which green frogs and forest creatures exhibited their natural graces. Now Vladimir is working on a new act, to be entitled the "Flying Rope-Walker."

His skill both as a rope-walker and as an actor, coupled with his vivid imagination, have made Vladimir Volzhansky, Merited Artiste of the R.S.F.S.R., one of the more popular Soviet Circus performers.

Vladimir Volzhansky created this trick. His partner looks very secure

However, Vladimir Volzhansky is also a teacher. Valentina Demina and Lev Osinsky, two well-known acrobats and rope-walkers, were once fledglings in his troupe. Volzhansky is now training his young daughter Marina, who recently graduated from secondary school.

1964

Weightlessness is something cosmonauts have discovered, too

The road to success is never easy

The aerialists look as if
they are going to fly
away

LEV OSINSKY, ROPE-WALKER

By V. Angarsky and A. Viktorov

Have you ever stopped to wonder that one of the most remarkable things about the circus is the very unusual nature of everything that goes on under the big top? The art of the circus is in itself unusual, and the performers are unusual people with unusual talents. Many of them have lived unsuspectedly heroic lives. One would think that trapeze artists and lion-tamers, as well as the daredevil riders, lead dangerous lives, indeed. But what about another form of circus art, that of the rope-walker who walks on his hands, for instance? The following is the true story of one such performer, Lev Osinsky of the Moscow Circus.

Lev began his circus career quite modestly when he was taken on in 1938 as one of a troupe of acrobats. However, young as he was, he had already set himself the distant goal of one day reaching the top. He was not the first, nor by far the only one, to have ever set himself such a goal, but not all of those who did had the will-power, the perseverance, or the true talent to succeed. Osinsky began by endless rehearsals. In two years' time he became a member of a top-rate acrobatic team directed by Nikolai Vol-zhansky. Their act, a pantomime in which Russian fairy-tale characters appeared, was known

"The Monument" is an unusual act

as "The Forest Fantasy." It combined rope-walking and various acrobatic tricks. Comical green frogs hopped, jumped, danced and walked on their hands in a "forest clearing." Lev was one of the "frogs." From then on he switched to rope-walking on his hands, an old and honoured form of circus rope-walking. It was popular in olden Russia where acrobats used to amaze the market crowds, amuse the nobles and fill the connoisseurs with awe and admiration. This art was practically forgotten by the turn of the century, and Lev Osinsky was one of the first to revive it. His was a difficult art, and he had to compete with such well-known rope-walkers as Nikolai Volzhansky, Mikhail Yegorov and Vladimir Yakovlev until they finally agreed he was the best. When Osinsky reached the top he began thinking of further means of improving his act, of creating a new type of act. However, the outbreak of war interfered with these plans. The young performer lost his left arm in the war. How could a one-armed man perform on his hands? One might recall the legends of composers gone deaf and artists who lost their eyesight. There was no question that their careers had come to an end. And yet, these men had carried on! As Lev Osinsky lay in his hospital bed, he recalled all the stories he had heard. What could an acrobat do if he was one-handed? Despite his grave doubts, he began to practise. From that moment on his confidence in himself and the possibilities that were open to him increased daily. The support and encouragement he received from his friends and colleagues were a major factor in his recovery. It took him a long time to learn to use his artificial arm, not simply as a handicapped veteran would, but in a very special way, as if filling the straps and metal with live muscle and nerves. At times this was truly torturous. He progressed from simple exercises for his left hand to more difficult ones, as if performing a series of tricks. His courage was unusual, and in time he returned to the circus and the tight-wire. However, his goal was not merely to achieve professional competence. Soon he was convinced that he had reached his pre-war level, that he was once again at the very top of his field. First his friends and colleagues noticed this, and then the audiences as well. His performances became more and more popular, he toured Poland, Yugoslavia, Greece, Belgium and Luxembourg. Not everyone knew they were witnessing a performance by a one-handed acrobat, but they all knew that here

166

was a performer of real talent. It is perhaps ironical that now that Osinsky was handicapped, he finally decided to realise his old dream of creating a romantic character. Not a dramatic one certainly, but a true circus hero. His inherent grace and the beauty of the composition made this possible. He was now a producer as well. The overall impression one receives from his performances is a harmony of movement and composition which one usually associates with the ballet. But this is a circus performance, a circus act in which Osinsky has planned and designed everything, from the special pedestal to the entirely new manner of presentation. Yes, this man is truly a hero.

Thus we see once again that the circus is a treasure-store of the unusual, a reflection of man's love for life, of his will-power, presence of mind and spirit. Thus we see that the people of the circus are a true match for their chosen art.

1964

VALENTINA
SURKOVA

By T. Podobedova

If you ask Valentina to tell you about an interesting event in her life she will probably recall, among others, the Sixth World Youth and Student Festival in Moscow. During the warm summer days of the Festival the streets, squares and parks of the city were filled with youths and girls, flowers and songs, and everywhere, in every language, one heard the words "Peace" and "Friendship"!

The ancient Moscow Kremlin, so magestic and solemn, became a place of wonderful parties and stirring meetings.

Valya recalls the ball at the Kremlin, the glitter and laughter and music. A dark-haired olive-skinned youth came up and waltzed her off. When the music ended, they became properly acquainted with the aid of a pocket dictionary, smiles and gestures. He was an Italian and worked in a shop, he liked music and sports, while Valya.... But we'll tell you about her later.

They walked over to a small bandstand where young people were competing in singing their native songs.

Valya looked at her companion and said: "Santa Lucia?" He nodded, and together they mounted the steps to the stage and sang the old Italian song, a Russian girl and an Italian youth who had met at the Festival.

Next we see them in the sports area. The contest there was much more difficult. A stout rope was attached to a crossbar very high above the ground. The one who could climb the rope without using his feet would win. Many young people tried their skill and, as the onlookers laughed and teased, they discovered they could not even climb half-way up it.

Then suddenly a slim, frail-looking girl in a pretty silk dress went over to the rope. In a flash she was at the top, touched the crossbar and came down hand-over-hand again. The young man was astounded. With great difficulty Valya found the words she needed to say: "I am a circus performer. Come to the circus tonight!"

The Moscow Circus had prepared a special Festival programme, entitled "Holiday of Youth." Taking part in the programme were the best circus performers of the Soviet Union. Valentina Surkova, an aerialist, was one of them.

There were three rounds in the contest to determine which acts would perform in Moscow. Fourteen of the top trapeze acts from various countries competed for first place. Valentina

The Big Top is always closer to Valya Surkova than the arena below.

but her heart is with her
audience

Surkova received the highest rating and won the gold medal and First Place Diploma.

Quite a few years have passed since then. The act she performed for the Youth Festival has become much more difficult. There are many new tricks, and the presentation has improved considerably.

Recently, Valentina Surkova's act once again began the programme of the Moscow Circus. In the glare of the powerful spotlights the lithe young acrobat is carried high up under the circus top. There is grace and beauty in her every movement.

Valentina performs at a dizzying pace. The tricks become more and more difficult as she rises higher and higher. This is the romantic flight of youth, captivating in its courage and true artistry. The tricks follow one another in close succession as she swings from a trapeze to rings, to a horizontal bar and loop. She does forward and backward bends on the rings, then a split and handstand. Suddenly, she seems to become suspended in a horizontal position, then she pivots 360° on one hand; this is followed by a leap to a horizontal bar and a series of turns, faster and faster, and faster—twelve in all!

This leads to the finale. Valentina grasps a loop with one hand and hangs suspended from it twenty metres above the ring. In an instant she assumes a horizontal position, having pulled herself up from hanging vertically by one extended arm. The audience applauds. But wait! She is repeating the trick, once, twice, three times, four times ... nine times in all! The suspense is too great. Swinging up for the last time she suddenly plummets down, still retaining her horizontal position, coming to her feet only at the very arena floor.

Circus fans return again and again to watch this unusual performance. In a very short time Valentina Surkova has become the country's top aerialist, known not only at home but abroad.

The Swedish press called her the Queen of the Air. *Die Junge Welt* (Berlin) wrote: "Surkova performs acrobatics in the air the likes of which no one has ever seen a woman do before and which one is not sure of ever seeing again." Success was the reward of long years of practice, a sincere love of and faith in the circus and the aid received from experienced teachers and performers of the older generation.

1964

LISIN
AND
SINKOVSAYA
By V. Angarsky
and A. Vikforov

Acrobatics is an ever-popular circus attraction having come down to us through the ages Countless generations of acrobats have perfected their skill in the constant search for new and more amazing tricks. Acrobats perform on a spring net, a spring-board and a trampoline. but the audience sees them mostly in the air; this is only natural, for flexibility, skill and flight are all closely related Acrobats have risen higher and higher. from the floor of the ring to trapezes, swings, etc. If an acrobat has a creative streak in him, he will try to find new and more modern ways of presenting his act

All this has a direct bearing on Viktor Lisin and Yelena Sinkovskaya of the Moscow Circus, who have spent much time and energy and used a lot of imagination in creating their original acrobatic act. In the process they have tried everything from a spring net to every other "earthly" device used to propel an acrobat into the air and decided against them all. From the very beginning they chose movement as the basis of their act, but movement in the air! How could it be made more interesting? Perhaps what they needed was an acrobatic apparatus. This is what finally formed the basis of their unique act.

This was the first interplanetary flight It took place in the circus

When audiences took their seats before a performance they usually noticed a strange contraption hanging under the circus top. Later, when the m.c. announced the next act to be Lisin and Sinkovskaya, the lights would go out. In the darkness, illuminated only by a single spotlight, a large metal torpedo slowly circled to the ground. They jumped aboard and began their difficult tricks on top of the moving torpedo, tricks which seemed all the more impossible, because they had no firm footing during the entire act. "The Flying Torpedo" was a popular favourite in Soviet circuses for many years.

Then 1957 marked a new chapter in world history, when a Soviet rocket ship took the first artificial earth satellite into orbit. Lisin and Sinkovskaya were as awed by this event as everyone else. However, there was just slightest tinge of sadness in their joy, for now their act would certainly seem shabby compared with such astounding scientific development. Thus, events in the outside world affected the small world of the circus. Lisin and Sinkovskaya did not want to lag behind the great world, in fact they wanted to reflect it in their act. There followed months of work, planning, calculating and rehearsing until the new act was ready, the one in which they now appear.

To the strain of "cosmic" music a heavy silvery rocket ship floats into the ring. In a way, we probably imagine that the first passenger rocket ship will look like this. It rises higher and higher, circling the ring until it is under the very top. In the bright glare of the spotlights a trapdoor opens and two people emerge. The rocket begins to circle faster and faster, it seems that it has left not only the circus but even the earth behind, while two fearless "astronauts" perform their bold and beautiful tricks atop it. The dynamic performance blends with the sight of the flying rocket and the whole unusual scene is one of man conquering the elements.

Lisin and Sinkovskaya are two of the best Soviet acrobats, their act is one of the best in the Moscow Circus. They have toured most countries of the world and everywhere they were applauded, both symbolically and for their own fearless performance. Their difficult tricks, done during the rocket's dizzying flight, are extremely dangerous. The act arrived in London in 1957 and there the performers discovered that the voltage in England was different than in the Soviet Union. At best, the motor would be ruined; the other possibility was that the speed would be increased to such a degree as to send the acrobats flying off the rocket. However, without a moment's hesitation, they decided to go on with the show. This was one time the mechanics were much more worried than the performers. As usual, the husband-and-wife team of Viktor Lisin and Yelena Sinkovskaya, both Merited Artistes of the R.S.F.S.R., was in top form. This circus family carries its honourable title nobly, for their rocket ship is in the vanguard of the Soviet circus.

1964

THE CIRCUS PRODUCER

By N. Zinovyev

Many circus fans would like to know what the circus producer does. They write letters, inquiring how circus performances are staged and what part the producer plays in pantomimes and other acts.

I have three letters before me, written at different times and in different countries.

"My friends and I have just seen the pantomime 'The Adventures of the Bear Leader and His Bear,' and were very impressed by what we saw," writes I. Arkadyev of the Leningrad Opera and Ballet Theatre. "It is a very successful combination of drama and circus tricks. Was everything in the pantomime staged by the producer? If his efforts are reflected in the actors' performances, who then can direct the four-legged characters? After all, the trained bear who plays Max gives an excellent portrayal of the hero of the pantomime. Who worked with the bear? Who went over the staging with him? Was it you, or was it the trainer Valentin Filatov who created the magnificent 'Bear Circus' which you included in the pantomime?"

Here is the second letter. I received it in Brussels while on tour at the World's Fair with the Soviet circus troupe. It is signed "Jacqueline from Ostend." "...There were thousands of people at the circus box office yesterday, all of them eager to be at the première of the Soviet circus. I was first in line and got the first ticket.

"...This evening I read *Le Soir* and found an article about your tour. I was especially interested in the following lines: 'There is real staging in the Soviet circus, just as in the theatre.' Please forgive me if I say that I do not fully understand the role of a producer in a circus programme which is composed of separate acts, created with great skill by the performers of your circus. What could a producer do here to be of help?"

Here is the third letter. It was written by Dr. F. Petrosyants of the Krasnaya Moskva Sanatorium, Sochi.

"I found your name in the circus programme next to the names of the performers, crediting you with producing the entire programme. I know what the duties of a producer are in the theatre, as I was a theatre doctor for many years, and I understand the work of a film producer, but I hope you won't mind my saying that I cannot understand what there is for a producer to do in a circus. True, there are times when I feel a producer has been consulted, most noticeably at the beginning of the performance when the entire troupe appears and during the various mass scenes. Then again, the producer probably helps the clowns in presenting their acts, jokes and ditties. But what about the very core of the programme, the true circus acts that include animals, what does a producer do there?"

Now I would like to tell you a bit about circus acts and pantomimes and how they are put together.

*   *   *

The scene is the Gorky Recreation Park during the tour of a circus from Sweden. The canvas Big Top swayed slightly on its four tall masts. Beyond the iron fence crowds were waiting to enter. At 8 o'clock sharp the lights in the arena went out. A lion-tamer appeared in a round iron cage with his lions. At a sign from the tamer the obedient beasts jumped from pedestal to pedestal in the dimly-lit cage. The circus performance had begun.

The next act was a woman aerialist. But why was there such a clatter of iron coming from the ring during the most difficult

177

Careful, now, it might bite!

and dangerous part of her act? We involuntarily tore our eyes from her and looked down. There we saw a great commotion, with attendants bustling about, dismantling the iron cage that had been used in the previous act. One's impression of her performance was shattered. Certainly this had robbed the trapeze artist of her well-deserved acclaim! Her exit soon after was sad, indeed, as she made her way through the crowd of attendants still busy in the ring and the elephants that were just entering.

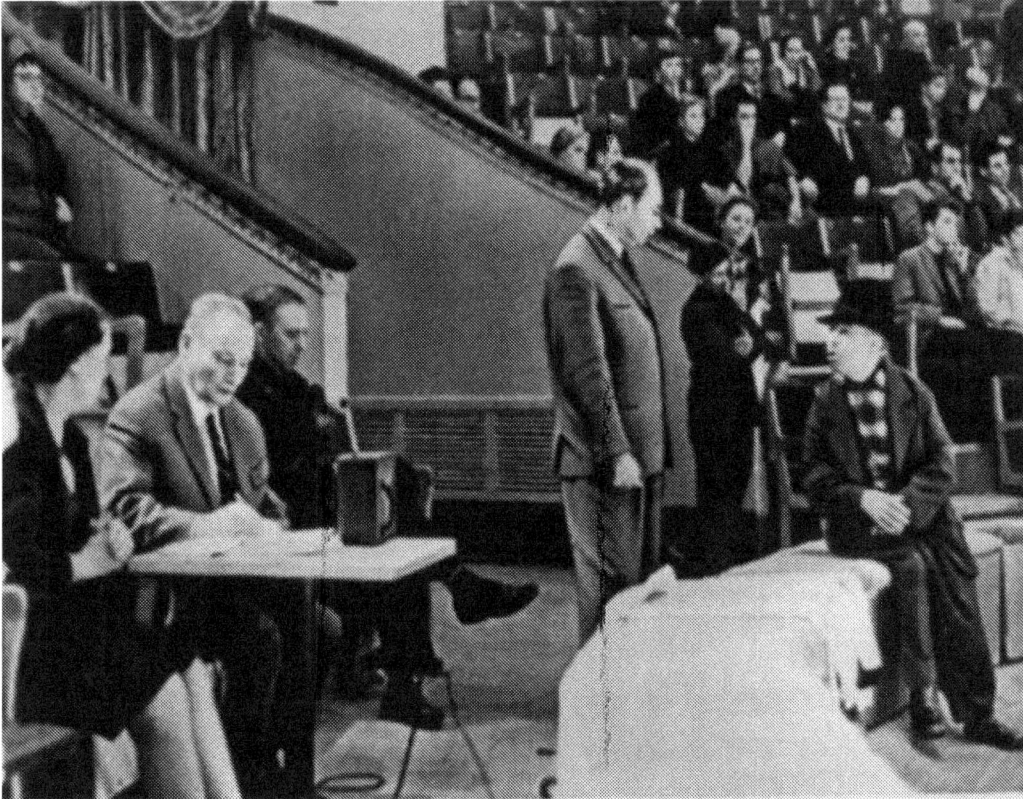

There were long pauses between the various acts. Why did they hang so heavily, as empty periods of time, why had they not been filled with action? Every now and then there were breaks in the programme. Did this not distract and bore the audience? Who should have seen to all these things? Would not a producer have solved these problems? What was needed here was imagination and something that would bind the various acts into a single, well-knit programme. Perhaps the acts should have been

Several clowns rehearsing together is very much like bedlam

Parade of the circus performers

reconstructed to eliminate the pauses; perhaps a clown should have been brought in to amuse the audience; perhaps.... Actually, there are so many things that could have been done if only one were to put one's mind to it.

Finally, it was intermission time. We now had a chance to exchange opinions. Though many of the acts were truly commendable, the question still remained: why was the general impression so uneven, why was there such a diversity in costume, why were the ring and the costumes so lacking in colour, in brightness?

There is only one answer: there was no producer to take care of all these matters. It is the producer who works out the programme according to a single theme, it is he who arranges for an artist to design the production. Together they draw up the plans of the settings. The artist also prepares sketches of the ring and the costumes. The producer plans the programme in a way to provide continuous action, with either clowns appearing in the pauses between the acts or other means unnoticeably put to use. The producer has the right to suggest changes in the acts on the programme, and, finally, it is he who invites a composer to create a special score for each act.

Soviet circus programmes usually begin with colourful mass prologues in which the entire troupe appears. As a rule, the text of the prologue is in verse. Its theme depends on the theme of the entire performance, but in general it reflects the wholesome nature of the Soviet circus and sets the spirit for the entire programme. The performance ends with a Grand Finale or epilogue in which once again the entire troupe appears.

Producers first appeared in the circus when stage directors became interested in this form of art in their search for new types of theatrical presentations in the first years after the Revolution. Circus tricks became accepted stand-bys in theatrical productions staged by Meyerhold, Tairov, Okhlopkov, Eisenstein and others.

Well-known stage directors took a liking to the vivacious, ever-popular art of the circus, they began experimenting, searching for something new in circus performances. The former Moscow Music Hall put on a series of interesting performances. Such talented writers and poets as Mayakovsky, Bedny, Afinogenov, Romashev, Ilf and Petrov, Katayev and Erdman began writing for the circus.

Grigory Alexandrov's popular film *Circus* was based on *Under the Big Top*, an original play by Ilf and Petrov, which had a successful run at the Music Hall. Many famous stage directors such as Petrov, Gorchakov, Akimov and Radlov, lent their talents to the circus.

A producer must keep track of everything that goes into a circus performance. Thus, for instance, in the comedy skits the clowns usually make fun of the preceding act, appearing in the pauses between acts. The tempo, uniformity and success of the entire production depend on the sequence of acts and clown's skits. This then is the role of a circus producer in a regular circus programme.

* * *

A circus spectacle is something else again.

There have been many of these in the history of the Soviet circus; for the greater part they have been pantomimes presented in the language of tricks and clowning, and sometimes dialogue as well. As a rule, they were satirical or comical in nature. The more successful circus pantomimes were "The Black Pirate" and "Makhno's Men," both staged by Williams Trucci, a wonderful producer and actor, and "The Taiga in Flames," staged by Petrov. "The Shot in the Cave," an aquacade and pantomime by Ostrovsky presented at the Leningrad Circus by one of our top directors, G. Venetsianov, Merited Artiste of the R.S.F.S.R., was of special interest. "The Adventures of the Bear Leader and Bear," written by N. Erdman and produced by N. Zinovyev, was first staged at the Leningrad Circus, and "Song of the Brave," produced by M. Mestechkin, was first presented at the Saratov Circus.

The circus producer, as the producer in a theatre, deals with a scenario which he then stages.

The circus producer consults with the artist and composer, he works with the actors, stages the production, conducts dress rehearsals, is in charge of lighting effects and must combine the whole into a single performance at the dress rehearsal.

The producer's work in creating a pantomime is complicated by the specific nature of this genre. Thus, in order to show a character's courage and skill, the performer turns to acrobatics. In general, the more use the producer makes of circus tricks, the more expressive and meaningful the action will be.

In the pantomime "Swords Clash" (produced by M. Volny), there is an ovation when a wounded horse kneels to let a wounded soldier climb to its back and then limps off-stage. The audience is just as amazed when (in the pantomime "The Adventures of the Bear Leader") a bear climbs up a column in pursuit of a whiteguard and grabs him by the pants, then climbs to a balcony, saves a woman and carries her down a rope to safety. This action, well within the boundaries of a

182

circus performance, could never have been attempted in a theatre. Here, too, it is the producer who directs the various scenes, while the animal-trainer rehearses them with the animals. The producer is not called upon to be an animal-trainer, acrobat, juggler or gymnast. But he must know the techniques of their performances. If he did not, he would never be able to offer them pertinent suggestions on the content of their act or the manner of presentation.

This, on the whole, is the producer's job in staging spectaculars and pantomimes.

* * *

The producer's most difficult job is to create a new act.

Anyone who has ever seen Valentin Filatov's "Bear Circus" has marvelled at the shaggy actors. Everyone considers Valentin Filatov, People's Artiste of the R.S.F.S.R., to be the sole creator of this world-famous act. But this is not so.

Many years ago I. Nemchinsky, a talented actor and producer, suggested that Filatov create an original sketch instead of his short bear act. In it the bears would perform in every circus genre. I. Fink, a writer, was called in to help with the script of the "Bear Circus" in which a real bear circus was to be presented in the ring, one in which there would be bear jugglers, aerialists, acrobats, rope-walkers, roller-skaters, bicycle riders and even a bear clown, a bear Karandash, as it were, who would fill in the pauses with fun. The bear clown would run around with a fire extinguisher, he would race along the railing on his hind legs, accompanied by a dog, he would take part in a boxing scene as the comical referee and as a coach with a pail and towel. He would also appear in a militiaman's uniform to make a stubborn bicycle-riding bear leave the ring.

Filatov began rehearsing. Some of the tricks did not turn out as planned, while others evolved in the course of the rehearsals. Nemchinsky, the producer, supervised the work. When the tricks had been mastered, Nemchinsky launched his own rehearsals, weaving the tricks into the settings, editing the script, paring it down to the bare essentials to keep up the fast pace.

A. Falkovsky designed the settings, the bears' costumes, the trainer's costume and the props.

Undoubtedly, Valentin Filatov did the lion's share of the work in the "Bear Circus," but the act would never have been what it is without the contributions of the producer and artist.

Most people have seen Margarita Nazarova's act in the film *The Tiger-Tamer*, where she appears with her group of trained tigers. Boris Eder, People's Artiste of the R.S.F.S.R., whose name is familiar to all circus fans, produced the act.

Boris Eder was originally an animal-trainer, but he showed great talent as a producer and eventually began writing the scripts for and staging his own animal acts.

A. Arnold produced Kio's famous magic reviews.

* * *

What part does the producer play in the various acts that make up a circus programme?

There is a generally accepted opinion that the performers themselves create their own acts. This is nearly correct, for there is probably no other form of entertainment so diverse in style and temperament as the circus. Each act is unique, each has its own technique which can be mastered only through much training and imagination on the part of the performer. The producer must have a knowledge of the essentials of a given genre, he must be able to visualise an act as it will finally appear and determine its composition.

Certainly, no circus producer knows everything. They usually specialise in several specific fields. Often, as in the theatre, the performers themselves become producers. Some graduate from theatrical institutes and receive degrees.

Unfortunately, very little has been written about the Soviet circus and hardly anything at all about the various problems which arise in staging circus performances.

Thus, no one but the performers themselves know that Williams Trucci is an outstanding circus producer. He is known as a bareback rider throughout the world, but he is also the creator of many acts, the most popular of which is "The Arabian Nights" pantomime.

Y. Kuznetsov, Merited Art Worker of the R.S.F.S.R., has dedicated his entire career to the circus, staging many programmes both in the Moscow and Leningrad circuses.

The whole world knows Oleg Popov, but few, indeed, know that his tight-wire act was produced by S. Morozov of the Moscow Circus School.

184

Much is being done in the field of clowning, satire and musical oddities, where many famed comedians and clowns work hand-in-hand with the circus producers.

Over the years Mikhail Rumyantsev (Karandash) has worked fruitfully with A. Fedorovich, G. Venetsianov, M. Mestechkin, and A. Arnold. Boris Vyatkin, Konstantin Berman, Mozel and Savich, all of whom are very versatile clowns, base their acts on various circus tricks staged by circus producers. Circus producers must have imagination, good taste, organisational abilities and a specific knowledge of the circus.

1960

COURAGE AND IMAGINATION
By N. Okhlopkov

In the many arguments and discussions on the contemporary theatre one rarely hears anything said of the circus and of the various changes that are now taking place within it. This is our common mistake. For if we take a closer look at the inner workings of these changes, we shall see positive proof of the relationship that exists between the circus and the theatre: we shall see that there are instances when the development of these two art forms lay very close together.

I had many occasions for becoming convinced of this. "Carnival in Cuba" was one, for the talented production, staged by M. Mestechkin, supplies much food for thought and for discussion on the future of the circus, although a cursory glance might not reveal more than the usual bright circus spectacular.

Undoubtedly, its catching, pulsing rhythms and tempo and its truly circus flavour are the

Boris Amarantov is four men in one. He's a juggler, gymnast, dancer and clown

two greatest merits of this pantomime. But this is only as it should be. The public watched with bated breath as the acrobats and gymnasts did their dizzying tricks, rejoicing at their success, laughing and applauding vigorously. I, too, held my breath in awe as I watched the unbelievable performances of the aerialists Surkova, Chiveli and Rytov, the acrobats Volkova and Sliva, the Tikhonovs, an animal-training team, the jumping Kasyanovs, Glozman and Karashkevich, two tight-wire walkers, and many other acts on the programme, which was a combination of skill and courage, grace and charm. Without these qualities there can be no circus. Yet this is not enough, this is not all that goes into a circus performance.

A closer look at the producer's work made it quite apparent that he wanted to broaden the horizons of the traditional circus performance, that he was guided by the truly deep, artistic principles of circus art.

As I watched the spectacle unfold, I recalled something that had no seeming relation to its theme. What I was thinking of was the famous actor Y. Yuriev playing Oedipus in the circus arena.

I recalled my own production of *The Iron Flood* at the Kiev Circus in 1934. The scene of the attack, the most powerful in the entire presentation, was best performed in the circus, as was the scene of the river crossing. The same held true for the scene in which a mother throws her child into a mountain gorge. The circus top seemed transformed into the sky overhead, and the applause was louder there than ever before.

I also recalled that the Euripides' *Medea* was originally intended as a circus performance. I thought of other plays which might conceivably be presented in the arena, such plays as Mayakovsky's *Mystery-Buff*, Cervantes' *La Numancia*, Aristophanes' comedies, Goethe's *Faust* and Dante's *Divine Comedy*.

188

Yuri Nikulin, a clown, can play serious roles as well

"Lunch, anyone?" says Leonid Yengibarov

What had brought on these thoughts during the performance? They were thoughts of the great driving force of the circus, of its unlimited possibilities, of its power of generalisation, which is paramount of all.

The circus can undertake any generalisation; in this truth lies its very essence. Conditionality is a welcome guest, and, what is most interesting, we accept it as reality in the circus. This makes for unusual scope and a diversity of means of expression that is capable of presenting profound thought and bold flights of fancy. This in turn makes it possible to create truly heroic personages as well as farcical ones, characters both pathetic and strikingly topical. There is reason why even in the most hackneyed of circus programmes one will always find death-defying courage and child-like, rollicking clowning. Life itself is reflected in this combination. We should remember that the great dramatists Shakespeare, Goethe and Dante always made use of startling contrasts between the high and the low. Death and laughter. Herein, also, are the circus's deep-lying, true points of contact with the theatre.

However, I would not like to create the impression that I want to transform the circus into a theatre, to deprive it of its own character.

The circus can put on plays and still remain a circus. It must at all costs avoid secluded action and unnecessary attention to detail, in a word, everything that can endanger its ability to present sweeping generalisations. In a way, the circus protects the inviolability of the power of generalisation bequeathed to the theatre. And if, at times, the theatre strives to camouflage its artistry, its "theatrical essence," through the natural and vividly realistic performances of its actors, the circus never conceals the fact that it presents art itself.

All these qualities must be retained. However, they must be combined with a truly artistic dramatic basis.

The circus needs a first-rate script, but it must not be set in juxtaposition to the pantomime. The pantomime is also an integral part of the circus and, as is known, can often be more expressive than words. There is reason why Charlie Chaplin began his career in the circus.

There are great possibilities for expansion in the circus, and one must not feel timid about letting them out, as a genie from a bottle. The circus script writers, producers, designers and the performers themselves must all take part in realising these new vistas. Poets, artists, composers and producers can all find new inspiration in the circus. And no one should ever say: "But you can't do this in the circus," or "You can't do that in the circus."

Much more can be done than we have come to expect. The search must be bolder, more courageous, for courage and imagination have been the motto of the circus from time immemorial!

1963

THE PAST RECALLED

CHEKHOV AND THE CIRCUS

By L. Gavrilenko

"Gilai, would you like to go to the circus today? If so, we'll expect you at 6:30, if not, lend me your season pass (Ivan and I are going)." This is a note written by Anton Chekhov to his friend, the writer Gilyarovsky.

"Chekhov and the circus?" the surprised reader will say. At first glance one might truly wonder what there is in common between Chekhov, that sensitive recorder of life, a man of deep and hidden thoughts and feelings, and the bright, eccentric spectacle we call the circus. Chekhov's contemporaries would not agree.

"Whenever Anton Pavlovich came to Moscow we went to Salamonsky's Circus. He loved the clowns and comedians and laughed like a child," wrote A. Vishnevsky, an actor of the Moscow Art Theatre and close friend of the author.

During Chekhov's voyages through Italy and France he went sightseeing, visited museums and galleries, and never once missed a chance to take in a circus performance.

Chekhov's interest in the circus was not merely a passing fancy. He dreamed fervently of the future well-rounded individual in whom "everything must be beautiful" and always admired the physical perfection, skill and courage of circus performers.

"Whenever I came to Melikhovo, Chekhov and his father, Pavel Yegorovich, would take me to see the horses grazing beyond the house. They would be very pleased if I showed them some riding tricks," Gilyarovsky wrote, who had been a circus performer in his youth.

It was this courage, skill and grace that made Chekhov so enamoured of the bright lights of the circus. He often associated his own good spirits and feeling of well-being with the circus.

However, Chekhov was never just another man in the audience. The circus, this tiny, unusual island of Russian life, attracted the writer in him from the very beginning.

In Chekhov's column "Fragments of Moscow Life" one also finds descriptions of circus life. Chekhov wrote this column for *Oskolki*, a magazine published in Petersburg, for nearly three years. There was more to it than social chatter, for he wrote of the social contradictions of his time. Once, a group of rich merchants on a spree had the trained pig that belonged to the famous clown Tanti roasted for them. In payment they tossed Tanti the tremendous sum of 2,000 rubles. This fact, as reflected in Chekhov's column, acquired its true social significance. The performer's humiliation, the trampling of his human dignity in a society where money was god, was by no means an unusual event at the time.

Chekhov was fascinated by the wit and satire of Vladimir Durov. Following is an excerpt from one of his articles, dated 1885, and written after he saw Durov perform.

"Moscow is terribly addicted to swinishness. Everything concerning swine, beginning with jellied suckling-pigs and horse-radish and ending with a swine triumphant, is greeted with open arms here. In Moscow, swines that are not only triumphant themselves but cheer the populace as well are held in especial esteem.... When the merchants 'gobbled up' Tanti's pig, the animal's place was not vacant long. The clown Durov ... trained another pig, thus taking the mournful Muscovites' minds from the deceased, who had but recently been digested in the merchants' stomachs. Durov's ingenue provides the audience with the greatest of aesthetic pleasures. She dances, grunts on command, shoots a pistol and, unlike so many Moscow oinkers, reads the newspapers. During Durov's last performance he presented, as one of his tricks, a pig reading the papers. It was offered a variety of newspapers but indignantly refused each of them in turn, grunting suspiciously all the while. At first, they thought that pigs hate publicity, too, but when the animal was offered a copy of *The Moscow Leaflet*, it oinked happily, wiggled its tail and, pressing its snout to the paper, shook its head excitedly. Such swinish delight gave Durov the right to make a public statement to the effect that all papers are intended for people, while the popular *Moscow Leaflet....* Avid readers of the *Moscow Leaflet* who were present at the time were not annoyed. On the contrary, they were delighted, and applauded the pig vigorously."

Chekhov continued in the same sarcastic vein, continuing the satire of the Russian clown, revealing its deeper significance. There rises from the pages of his column the symbolic image of a swine triumphant, the embodiment of the dark epoch of the 80s.

Chekhov was quick to notice the purely business-like, mercenary nature of many of the "sports and circus" performances at Lentovsky's famous Hermitage Gardens.

"From all corners of the world," Chekhov wrote in his column, "people walk and run to Moscow in quest of the prizes: all sorts of 'Austrian officers,' the famous sprinter who ran races in the presence of His Highness the Turkish Sultan, human birds, human snakes, human scorpions. All the hotel rooms and every nook and cranny are now occupied by these talented individuals, so close to the heart of all Muscovites."

In 1884, Chekhov wrote *In Bad Society*. In the second edition the title was changed to *Kashtanka*. There are two versions of the origin of the story's theme. In the first, Laikin, the publisher of *Oskolki*, insisted that it was he who had told Chekhov about a dog named Kashtanka. In the second, Vladimir Durov, in his book *My Animals*, gives a detailed description of an event that happened to him and which he later related to Chekhov:

"Kashtanka was a young chestnut-coloured dog, the first of my trained dogs. Before I got her she belonged to a poor cabinetmaker. Kashtanka was lost, she had lost her master and finally ended up with me. The story of this dog served as the basis for A. P. Chekhov's story *Kashtanka*, which he heard from me. I remember the time I first saw Kashtanka as if it were yesterday. It was winter, and it was snowing heavily. A small chestnut dog pressed close to the door of my house, whining helplessly, not knowing which way to go or where to seek warmth. The snow kept coming down, covering it from

196

head to tail, transforming it into a white shapeless mound with two large sad eyes.

"The dog was tired and sleepy. Suddenly, somebody pushed the door open. The dog jumped up and saw a short, clean-shaven man in an overcoat. This, of course, was me. The dog looked at me through the snowflakes on its eyelashes and probably sensed that I meant no harm. I brushed the snow from its back and called it after me. The dog came in and remained in my house thereafter. I began training it. Soon it showed such progress that it began performing in the circus with my other four-legged and feathered actors. Once, however, Kashtanka was the cause of a great commotion in the middle of our act. Kashtanka was going through her paces when she suddenly stopped and looked up to where a familiar voice had called to her. The cabinetmaker, her former master, had one of the balcony seats. Ignoring the crowd and my command, the dog scampered up through the rows to her former master."

It is difficult to say which of the two stories served as the basis of Chekhov's story. However, there can be no doubt that Chekhov "borrowed" Vladimir Durov for his clown. Durov was the most popular clown in the Russian circus and Chekhov was personally acquainted with him.

The description of the clown in Chekhov's story, the "short, round man with a clean-shaven plump face," is a true portrait of Durov. However, what is most important is not the portrait resemblance, but a resemblance in character and attitude. In describing his clown, Chekhov reveals the noble traits of the wonderful performer and innovator. He has created a man of great spiritual beauty and revealed his kindness, gentleness and true love of animals. He speaks of the work of a circus performer as of a true art form, based on persistent and inspired toil. The gentle humour of this personage makes him more likeable still.

Chekhov does not seem to bring his character into direct contact with the difficulties of life, but anyone who has read the story will recall the clown's sadness and loneliness. Herein lies the deeper meaning of the story, the bitter life of a circus performer in tsarist times.

Thus in the truly humane traditions of Russian literature did Chekhov approach one of the lesser themes of his work, the theme of the circus.

1960

A. KUPRIN, CIRCUS FAN

By N. Verzhbitsky

When I once asked Kuprin what the source of his undying love for the circus was, he answered without a moment's hesitation:

"Well, you see, I'm a hereditary animal-trainer. My uncle, a small Narovchat land-owner, was famous throughout Penza Gubernia for his ability to break in the half-wild Bashkir horses. He was a Tatar by birth and loved horse racing, wrestling and any other kind of *sabantui*, that is, any type of popular festivity with dancing, rope-walking or archery, where the strongest, most skilled and cunning are awarded prizes. Alas, all my uncle's artistic endeavours ended in nought, and he died a poor man. I will probably die a beggar, too. But this does not frighten me, for even though I go hungry, I will have many good memories. Do you know the tale about the pebbles on the beach?"

"No, I don't seem to recall it."

"It's a very short but convincing story. I heard it in Tiflis. An extremely wealthy man lost all his treasures in a single day. Then he went to live in a fisherman's hut on the seashore. He would sit on the beach for hours, watching the waves, fingering the pebbles, recalling his diamonds and pearls. 'These are also stones,' he mused. 'They have also been created by nature. Many of them are very beautiful but, most important, my soul is at peace, for no one will take them from me, no one will envy me for having them.' "

"On the Other Side," a story in which Kuprin recalls his own adventures, is about a junior lieutenant named Alexandrov who, just for fun, mounts a lame old one-eyed horse and rides up a flight of stairs to a restaurant on the second floor. While in the saddle he drinks a glass of brandy and rides down again, where he is greeted by a crowd of enthusiastic onlookers.

"You might say this was simply the stunt of a bored officer. Was it really just a stunt? If you think so, try to teach a one-eyed horse to climb a flight of stairs and come back down as well! The circus trainers and riders I know say this is one of the most difficult tricks to do."

When Kuprin was a youth in the Cadet Corps and later at the Junker Military Academy, he was known as a gymnast and dancer and excelled at formation marching.

Kuprin was six years old when an older boy of eleven came to visit relatives in the house on Kudrinka, in Moscow, where he lived with his mother. The boy, who knew various circus tricks, grew up to be the famous clown and animal-trainer Anatoly Durov. Little Anatoly took Sasha Kuprin to a back corridor, so that no one would see them, and showed him how he could jump, do somersaults, make faces and do impersonations. When Kuprin was away at a boarding-school several years later he would always go to the circus or the zoo on Sundays, preferring to spend the day watching the animals and observing their habits to playing with his friends at home. When he was ten years old and at the Rumyantsev Home, Kuprin was seized with the fantastic idea that he could fly if he jumped very quickly over a skipping-rope. He decided to see if the idea would work and climbed up a pole in the gymnasium, flipped the rope and jumped over it. Alas, he could not fly!

When Kuprin was a middle-aged man, he suddenly became fascinated with juggling. If one happened to be having dinner with him at the time, he would be surprised to see Kuprin suddenly toss an empty plate across the table with great accuracy; there it would be picked out of the air quite skilfully by one of his guests, who would naturally turn out to be a professional juggler.

In Kiev, Kuprin became acquainted with the famous wrestler Ivan Poddubny, who at the time was only a wrestler. Kuprin

The clown Jacomino surprised Kuprin during a friendly chat

prevailed upon him to take up classic wrestling and Poddubny later became World Champion, a title he retained through many international tournaments.

Kuprin took part in organising the Kiev Athletic Society, and as a lightweight wrestler he met with many formidable opponents. Later Kuprin became acquainted with Ivan Lebedev, organiser of the world wrestling championship meets in Petersburg's Modern Circus. Kuprin was often a judge at these matches. Many were the times during difficult or puzzling situations when the noisy and demanding balcony fans would protest against Lebedev's ruling. They would shout: "Get Kuprin! Let Kuprin be the judge!"

Then the famous writer would get up and say, pointing to the referee:

"My friends, don't shout! He's right!"

And the noise would subside.

Ivan Zaikin was a handsome, powerful circus strong man. He began his career by working with weights, pulling iron chains apart and bending steel crowbars over his neck. Kuprin also persuaded him to try his luck at classical wrestling. Besides, he got Zaikin interested in aviation. In Odessa, Kuprin and Zaikin were one of the first teams in Russia to fly a biplane. It flew about half a kilometre and then came crashing to the ground. From then on Kuprin became an avid aviation fan.

In 1910, as he watched the first non-stop Petersburg-Moscow flight in Russia getting under way, he noted wrathfully that this wonderful undertaking had been put in the hands of men who did not consider aviation to be of great national importance but merely a new source of amusement.

"Aviation has become stylish," he wrote. "Just as spiritualism, hypocrisy, a false interest in sports, and chiefly in sports clothes, have all become stylish. The gilded idiots have found it necessary to latch on to this tremendous undertaking."

At the time, the Italian clown and gymnast Jacomino was first appearing in the Modern Circus. Soon he became a frequent visitor at Kuprin's Green House in Gatchina. He tried to talk the writer into going to Italy and promised to be his guide there. Kuprin finally did set out for Italy, but when he arrived his friend was gone. Jacomino had just left for an unexpected engagement in Paris. All was not lost, for the result of this trip were Kuprin's wonderful travel notes, *The Azure Coast*.

*Ivan Zaikin, the famous wrestler,
swooped the writer off his feet*

It is unlikely that any other writer in the world devoted so much attention to the circus.

Kuprin's first short story, "Allez," of the proud love of a young circus acrobat, appeared in the 90s and drew an excited response from Lev Tolstoi.

While staying with Chekhov in Yalta in 1901, Kuprin wrote "At the Circus" which was enthusiastically acclaimed both by Tolstoi and Chekhov. Following is an excerpt from a letter Kuprin wrote to his friend L. Yelpatyevskaya.

"The theme is not too involved, but what breadth of action there is in it: the circus in the daytime, during rehearsals, in the evening, during the performance, the argot, the customs, the costumes, a wrestling match, the tense muscles and beautiful poses, the excitement of the crowd, etc. When I first thought of this yesterday, my hands turned cold from happiness. I did a dance round the room singing: 'I'll write it, I'll write it, I'll write it!' "

In a letter to Chekhov, dated 1903, Kuprin wrote:

"In our enlightened times it is considered shameful to confess a love for the circus, but I am courageous enough to do so."

In "The White Poodle" Kuprin writes of a little travelling circus that consisted of an old organ-grinder, a boy acrobat and a trained poodle. This is a story with deep social content, written with moving simplicity. It is one of the favourite stories of children everywhere. "The White Poodle" has gone through innumerable printings and translations.

Three of Kuprin's other famous circus stories are "Olga Sur," "Lighter Than Air" and "Crimson Blood."

Kuprin dreamed of a Russian circus, of a school of Russian circus performers with a repertoire that would be characteristic of the ingenuity and wisdom of the peoples inhabiting Russia.

"Will I ever live to see the day," he said, "when, on a circus poster, instead of foreign, and often invented names, one will find the names Ivanov, Gebitullin, Dadvadze and Sidorenko? I know they will create a repertoire no worse, and certainly much better and more original than the foreigners have, because our muscles are stronger, fate has not by-passed us with courage, and we have patience enough and laughter! Oh, we can laugh better than anyone in the world, because our laughter is of a very special kind."

1960

MAXIM GORKY'S IMPRESSIONS OF THE CIRCUS

By A. Lebedeva

"I like the circus and its performers, people who calmly risk their lives every day."

MAXIM GORKY

Maxim Gorky was drawn to the circus all his life, as is evident from his own words, his writing and the recollections of his contemporaries.

Gorky first went to the circus when he was eight or nine years old. He speaks of his passion for the circus in his childhood and youth in several of his autobiographical works. Gorky relates how Mishka, a boy from the icon-painters' shop is enchanted by a circus clown ("Shake-up", 1898). He tells us how Mishka, his face white from the strain, sat without a sound and from time to time shuddered from a desire to go tumbling across the ring in a bespangled costume. Nothing could dispell that impression. When the boy lay down to sleep on a pile of straw in the corner of the yard the stars shining in the sky reminded him of the gold spangles on the clown's costume. He began early next morning telling everybody in the workshop about the circus performance and gave them an imitation of the clown—and this saved him from the usual slaps and kicks.

And in the evening, when Mishka, after a soul-destroying "shake-up," is lying in bed, the bright colours of the icons remind him of the previous evening at the circus.

"And he sees the circus ring and he is in it. . . . The thunder of applause encourages him . . . full of admiration at his own agility, proud and happy, he leaps high into the air and flies away amid a roar of approval from the audience, flies away with a fluttering heart . . . to be awakened on earth by a sharp kick."

The impressions he received from the circus, "as beautiful and wonderful as a dream," were very different from those which had "hurt him in childhood by their cruelty and filth." The circus was but one of the many sources which awakened the creative talents of the future writer.

In his autobiographical book *My Apprenticeship* he recalled his days in the icon shop: "Excited beyond all measure, I would begin to retell and act out the ideas that had suddenly come to me, for I wanted so greatly to make the people truly happy in a free, light-hearted way.

" 'Maximich, you take yourself off to the circus or the theatre, you'll make a good clown,' the icon-painter Zhikharev said approvingly."

Gorky actually wanted to become a circus performer, but this venture ended in failure. He wrote of the episode in a story entitled "In the Theatre and at the Circus."

The circus beckoned in many ways. "Everything I saw in the arena blended into something triumphant, where skill and strength confidently celebrated their victory over mortal danger."

The world of the circus opened up before Gorky in the books he read at the time. Most notable was *The Brothers Zemganno* by Edmond de Goncourt. This is what Gorky said of it: ". . . My hands shook with pleasure at reading this book. I wept aloud when I read of the unfortunate acrobat, his legs broken, crawling up to the attic, to where his brother was practising his favourite art."

The memoirs of Upilio Faimali, an Italian lion-tamer, was another book that left a lasting impression on Gorky. Faimali was a very strong and courageous man. Born a peasant, he came to the circus by himself at the age of eleven, there to remain and become a skilled and fearless bareback rider. Later,

205

he became an animal-trainer and, finally, a lion-tamer, the crowning achievement of his career. Faimali had 120 animals, 32 of them lions, which was then considered very unusual. Faimali gave his show in the biggest cities of Britain, Austria, Germany, France, Spain, Belgium, and Holland; he was also in Russia, in St. Petersburg.

This unusual choice of profession, the lion-tamer's courage in the face of grave and constant danger, and man's power over the king of the beasts, were certainly thrilling.

Gorky later wrote of the books he was devouring at the time: "There are people who know how to live so fascinatingly and grandly, as no one else knows how to live."

When Gorky acquired a first-hand knowledge of circus life, he came to appreciate its other qualities as well, mainly, the strong feeling of comradeship and mutual responsibility that existed among circus performers. He recalled the words of a circus acrobat: "Thank God, we circus people live happily together! Our work is so dangerous that we must take care of each other." In recalling his childhood impressions of the circus Gorky noted that circus performers were unlike ordinary people both in appearance and conduct.

In "The Shake-up" Gorky wrote of a boy named Misha who was very displeased at seeing the glittering clown dressed in an ordinary suit after the performance, for this had changed him into an ordinary person.

In "The Hero" (1915), he wrote: "When life is unattractive and as dirty as an old cluttered ruin, one has to cleanse and brighten it with the means provided by one's soul and one's will, by the power of one's imagination and adorn it with a shining sheath of youthful romanticism."

Thus the writer stressed his own romantic attitude towards the vagaries of life. This is also characteristic of his attitude towards the circus and its people during his childhood and youth.

Early in his literary career Maxim Gorky worked on the *Samara Gazette*, the *Nizhegorodsky Leaflet* and *Odessa News*. In his articles he often took up the question of popular amusements and the circus, side-shows and public fist-fights in particular.

In speaking of the circus as a necessary and true art form, Gorky condemned all that was crude and unaesthetic, censuring the difficult and dangerous acts which were intended to whet the jaded appetites of the bourgeois public.

Gorky protested against "the crudest nonsense" of the circus, which had performers breaking stones on each other's heads with mallets, swallowing umbrellas and swords or burning tar, eating galoshes and walking barefoot over nails. In another article he wrote with indignation of the heroes of the day, clowns and wrestlers such as Abs, Moore, Foss and others.

"All these 'world-renown', 'unconquerable' and unbelievably stupid wrestlers are also Lilliputs, all of them have tiny heads on massive bodies, their eyes are dull, their expressions wooden. It is the duty of the press to make the public realise that all these giants and Lilliputs, clowns, magicians and three-legged freaks are neither rarities nor the result of creative art. They are victims artificially nurtured and especially provided for the public."

Gorky retained this unbending attitude towards all forms of amusement which aroused man's basest instincts.

He returned to this topic in one of his travel articles, "In the Kingdom of Boredom," one of a series entitled *In America* (1906). He wrote with wrath of the popular pastimes of Coney Island which also included a circus, a "match" between a lion-tamer and his animals, etc.

Taking into consideration the great popularity of the circus as an art form, Gorky wrote in his articles of the 90s of transforming the circus into a "sensible," "educational" form of amusement. At this time he was greatly taken up by the idea of setting up a people's theatre. It is common knowledge that in 1897 Gorky organised a rural theatre in the village of Manuilovka with a troupe recruited from among local peasants. The writer himself took part as both actor and producer. In 1903, a popular theatre was opened in Nizhny Novgorod, largerly due to the active interest displayed by Gorky.

Gorky was an ardent propagandist among theatre people of the idea of creating a people's theatre, we are told by the actor N. I. Skobolshchikov-Samarin, the organiser of the theatre co-operative in Nizhny Novgorod. He suffered a number of failures, but after his talk with Gorky he organised a series of popular shows in Astrakhan.

Gorky's views concerning the people's theatre, his notes on the importance of mass cultural and educational measures, were closely bound up with the Communist Party's policy on questions of the cultural education of the masses even before the October Revolution.

The legal Party newspapers—*Zvezda* (1910-1912) and *Pravda* (1912-1914) carried regular articles on literary and art themes and raised the question of the educational value of popular entertainments.

Ivan Filatov, the famous animal-trainer who died in 1956, recalled that during the 1903-1904 season Gorky was a frequent visitor at his show in Moscow, where, in the course of twelve years, Gorky's close friend A. Orlov, a well-known Volga folk singer, worked with Filatov. "Once," Filatov recalled. "when we were talking, Gorky said: 'I love this popular form of amusement to distraction.' "

Gorky's play *The Lower Depths* was presented in Filatov's fair booth instead of the usual circus pantomime. Gorky cut the play especially for this presentation, leaving only the most important scenes, and edited it together with his friend Orlov. Filatov played the Baron.

The play was very successful, and the first rows were all bought up by the "clean" public. Filatov recalled that Gorky always enjoyed these performances.

One of the characteristic traits of the Russian circus was its satirical nature. Gorky greatly admired the political satirist Anatoly Durov, a wonderful representative of the Russian school of clowning and animal-training, he valued the social content and significance of Durov's performances and his personal friendship with the clown.

Gorky was also interested in comedians and circus clowns, and after a performance he liked to exchange opinions with his friends.

In Gorky's recollections we find the following observation: V. I. Lenin "laughed readily and contagiously as he watched the clowns and comedians" at the Music Hall in London; how interesting it was to hear him speak of this form of comedy as a specific type of circus art: "There is a kind of satirical or sceptical attitude to the generally accepted, there is a desire to turn it inside out, to change it a bit and show the illogical nature of the ordinary. It is very involved, but interesting!"

208

V. I. Lenin considered the essence of circus comedy to be its satire on everyday life, its sceptical attitude towards bourgeois reality.

The scenario of *The Hard-Worker Wordflow* (1920), written for the Theatre of Popular Comedy was the result of Gorky's desire to use the art and satire of the circus in dealing a body blow to the shortcomings that still stood in the way of establishing a new way of life in a socialist society. There were both circus performers and actors in the troupe of the theatre and clowning and acrobatics were usually a part of the productions. Often, the leading roles would be given to such well-known circus performers as G. Delvari, a clown and acrobat, or Alexandrov-Serge, a rider and trapeze artist.

Gorky met with many of the circus performers before the play went into production.

The Hard-Worker Wordflow is a one-act play named for the main character, a petty official and a lazy good-for-nothing who is armed with a complete arsenal of super-revolutionary words and phrases.

After one of the rehearsals according to a script provided by Gorky, the actors were invited to his house, and, in the discussion that followed, the writer stressed the theme again: "It is actions, not words, that count."

P. Pavlenko, a well-known writer, in his memoirs recalls Gorky's interest in the circus. "Visiting the Moscow Circus one day, he was displeased at some sort of 'aquatic pantomime' and immediately got together a group of writers to write a 'review.' Some tried to talk him out of it. After all, what a combination: Gorky and the circus! They found this to be both trivial and funny. But as far as he was concerned, there were no such things as great or small themes, as worthy and unworthy genres."

Gorky was aware of the many faces of circus art. He felt its major assets were the courage, skill and physical beauty of the performers. This he considered to be the result of intensive physical training, so necessary for the harmonious development of the individual, of a person who lived for his work, and the creation of great cultural treasures.

1958

STANISLAVSKY'S LOVE OF THE CIRCUS

By A. Anastasyev

Stanislavsky's world of art is boundless. The great feat of his life was the creation of the Moscow Art Theatre, and his "Collected Works" were his 30 roles and the more than 50 plays he staged at the Art Theatre. Among them were Chekhov's masterpieces, as well as *The Lower Depths*, *Dr. Stockman*, *The Burning Heart*, *Armoured Train 14-69* and *Dead Souls*. As Gorky said to Stanislavsky, "Part of your work is concealed behind the curtain, a part which I especially value and admire: what a great and sensitive master you are in discovering new talents, what a skilled jeweller in educating and polishing them!" There was also his reform of the opera, the 8 volumes of his works, a priceless collection of experience and ethics, a manifesto of truth in art.

An actor's art is shortlived, as it lies within the boundaries of his lifetime. Stanislavsky refuted this bitter but just concept and not only because the characters he created (as was the case with many another great actor) were handed down in memory from one generation to the next. Stanislavsky discovered the laws of acting, he created a "system" which retained for ever his own vital stage experience and the experience of all that was progressive in the theatre "Like a prospector, I can pass on to my descendants not my toil, my searching, deprivation, joys and disappointments, but only the precious ore I have mined," Stanislavsky wrote. "In my artistic field this ore was the result of a search that lasted my entire lifetime, it is my so-called 'system,' the method of acting I have come upon which makes it possible for an actor to create the character of his role, to reveal the life of the human spirit in it and to project it naturally on the stage in a beautiful, artistic manner."

One sometimes hears that Stanislavsky's "system" belongs solely to the Art Theatre, where it was born. This is a great delusion. The "system's" great power lies in the fact that its laws, if one is to understand them artistically, comprise the basis of every actor's art, no matter in which play or in which character he appears to the audience. This is true not only of actors in the theatre, but in films, variety shows and the circus as well.

Following is an excerpt from a letter Stanislavsky wrote to the Moscow Music Hall in 1933: "Who now doubts the fact that in your field the actor's work can reach the heights of true art. There is good reason why the famous political clown* drew all the government officials and representatives of the various parties to the circus whenever he appeared. There is reason why the famous Tanti-Bedini is, in my estimation, the only representative of the truly grotesque, one of the most difficult types of art in which only the basic and nothing superfluous is necessary. Naturally, in your field, as in ours, there are the lowly hacks with whom one must fight and who must be mercilessly done away with. But there are many true artists among you whom I greet with all my heart."

There are many such true performers in the Soviet circus. One can only hope that all performers, no matter what their field, will acquire the truthfulness, the natural and beautiful artistic manner towards which the great master of the stage blazed the way.

1963

* Vitaly Lazarenko.

MERRY EVENINGS AT THE ART THEATRE

By V. Gotovtsev

Stanislavsky loved all forms of art and was a circus fan from early youth. He often reminded us of the circus performer's difficult and responsible work, one that can serve as an example for actors of the stage. He believed that the skill of the acrobats and riders, the courage and presence of mind of the animal-trainers and the ability to concentrate were all worthy of imitation.

In calling upon us to improve our technique, to master the art of mimicry, gesture, plasticity and co-ordinated movement on stage, Stanislavsky referred to the circus, where there were wonderful examples of all these qualities and discipline in art. It is common knowledge that the slightest deviation from the set order of most circus acts can lead to tragedy.

During the comic circus performances of the "Merry Evenings" at the Art Theatre Stanislavsky took the part of the circus manager, and the Manager's bell was law to all those participating in the show.

A great number of circus parodies were put on during the 1910-1911 season. The famous wrestler Van-Reel was present at one such performance. N. Podgorny, one of the actors in Stanislavsky's Studio, put on a mock wrestling match with him. We set up an "arena" on the stage and the Manager (Stanislavsky) took his place at one of the entrances. He was dressed in shiny black knee-boots, breeches, a vest and a top hat. This was his childhood dream (as we later learned from his book *My Life in Art*) come true. He held a staff and, as the emblem of his high office, a bell. The finishing touch of the threatening figure he presented was his stern gaze from under his bushy black brows. Actually, he was impersonating Albert Salamonsky, then director of the Moscow Circus.

The circus performance commenced. There was a "horse act" in which the "horses" were actresses of the Art Theatre, and Olga Knipper-Chekhova was one of them. At the barely audible tinkle of the Manager's bell the "horses" changed pace, did various turns and, in conclusion, bowed to the audience and trotted offstage. Next to appear was the Groom, dressed as a doorman. This was the famous Ivan Moskvin. He carried a large dustpan and broom and swept the ring.

I think that Stanislavsky's love of the circus prompted the young Studio actors to put on several skits entitled "The Circus" in which the participation of circus "animals" was mandatory. These skits were part of the Studio programme for quite a while; they made the students observe the ways and habits of animals. Stanislavsky was true to himself, for he wanted the actor to have a close affinity with life and nature, for therein lay the key to an understanding of realistic art.

1962

FOND RECOLLECTIONS

By Alisa Koonen

I have loved the circus ever since I was a child. My first impressions were very vivid. In my memory, as in a picture album, are recollections of Vladimir Durov's "Animal Railway," of the bold political satire of Anatoly Durov, the magnificent stables of the Russian trainers Nikitin, Mangelli and Leri, and of the colourful circus pantomimes. It was the turn of the 20th century and circus performances were enveloped in great pomp and circumstance. The competing managers and directors spared no effort to outdo each other, to amaze the public by the magnificent adornment of the horses, by fake jewels that glittered brilliantly, by the fabulous ostrich trimmings on the costumes and by the use of dazzling lights.

This "magnificence" often overshadowed the performers' excellent showmanship. However, the overall impression of these spectaculars was awe-inspiring, fascinating and colourful. It could not but hypnotise me at the time.

No wonder then that each new visit to the circus fired me with a desire to be like the fearless gymnasts, the graceful bareback riders, the exquisite tightrope-walkers and the temperamental dancers that were a part of every performance.

My first public appearance took place soon after a visit to the circus, when I decided to try my skill on a tightrope. I recall I was spending the summer in the country and pretended that our cottage was a circus arena. With this as my starting point, it was easy to construct a makeshift stage from two stools and an ironing board. I then strung a heavy cord between them, put on a pair of crimson trousers, took up an umbrella and, balancing carefully, began my trip across the rope. From then on I began practising in earnest, devoting my time to gymnastics and dancing as well. All this helped me to become light and graceful, and I was always ready to perform at the drop of a hat. I was fifteen that autumn and took the entrance examinations at the Actor's Studio of the Moscow Art Theatre. The members of the examining committee (Maxim Gorky was one of them and seemed huge and melancholy to me) were sitting in judgement in the theatre lobby. When it was my turn, I took a flying jump to the little stage where I was to recite a poem, and no one but a circus performer could have appreciated it. Vladimir Nemirovich-Danchenko probably thought I was still a baby and said rather sternly: You had better stay at home a while longer and read some good books."

However, they accepted me, and this in spite of the fact that there were no vacancies.

Then began my unforgettable years of study at the Studio and, later, my work at the theatre under the direction of Stanislavsky. He himself loved the circus and would often repeat half-seriously: "The circus is the best place in the world." And that is why, several years later, a large part of one of the Art Theatre's "Merry Evenings" was devoted to circus clowning.

That evening the theatre was transformed into a large carnival hall with tables set up in the dress circle. L. Geltzer, a well-known actress of the Bolshoi Theatre, kept busy selling champagne at one of the stands. Meanwhile, a "circus" programme was in full swing on stage, with the entire troupe of the Moscow Art Theatre, headed by Stanislavsky, Kachalov, Moskvin and Olga Knipper-Chekhova, performing.

Fyodor Shalyapin took part in the performance, appearing as a circus strong man.

The young students often had the leading roles in these "Merry Evenings." Thus it was that I appeared with Stanislavsky. He played the part of a horse-trainer, while I was a

Alisa Koonen proved that women could clown too

Spanish bareback rider. My "steed" was a spirited white wooden horse. It was life-size and secured to a revolving disc. I was to go through all my tricks, smiling the traditional smile, moving in a direction opposite to that of the horse. It was then that my love of the circus stood me in good stead. The act was a difficult one, and we had rehearsed it for quite a while. In the mornings in a part of the theatre lobby walled off with sheets of plywood, Stanislavsky would practise the difficult art of wielding a cane under the watchful eye of a professional circus horse-trainer. One could hear the snapping of a whip and the ever-present "*hup!*" pronounced in the tone of a command by the diligent pupil.

I will never forget my feeling of despair during the dress rehearsal, when it suddenly became apparent that the rider's costume rented for the occasion from the circus wardrobe was too heavy and cumbersome and quite unsuited for the light humour and mischievous spirit of my performance. I kept tripping on the hoops, while the stiff bodice, encrusted with a mass of glass beads, was suffocating.

Maria Lilina, Stanislavsky's wife and one of the Moscow Art Theatre actresses, came to my rescue, as she had done so many times before for young actresses in distress. From the bottom of her "magic" trunk she brought forth a wide gauze cape covered with red sequins. She draped it around me like a skirt, winding a bright scarf around me for a bodice with a large bow on the side. To complete my costume, she stuck a huge red cloth poppy in my hair and then clapped her hands with pleasure. "That's just what you want, something light and amusing," she said. I felt very secure in my new costume and ran excitedly towards my "steed." The improvised skirt fluttered about me as was only proper. My act was included in the programme and was a success. The horse "galloped" along the stage, while I did my breath-taking tricks, bending so low at times that my long braids dragged on the floor. Stanislavsky cracked his whip with obvious pleasure. He had on a huge black moustache and was made up to resemble a Spaniard. Indeed, he looked exactly like the formidable trainer he was impersonating.

Several years later it was my good fortune to work with A. Tairov, People's Artiste of the R.S.F.S.R., a wonderful director and circus lover. The troupe of actors working with him at the Kamerny Theatre belonged to different schools and directions of acting. Tairov, who dreamed of a composite theatre. strived to combine and blend the various elements of harlequinade. tragedy, operetta, pantomime and the circus.

He believed that a new type of actor, one who was equally at ease in any genre, could become the driving force behind such a theatre.

"The emotional gesture, the emotional form, is the theatrical synthesis without which there can be no contemporary theatre and in which all spheres of stagecraft are organically blended," Tairov said. "Thus. in one and the same presentation all the elements which are now artificially separated—words, singing, pantomime, dancing and even the circus—will blend in harmony, becoming, as a result, a unified and monolithic theatrical presentation." Tairov demanded that his actors have not only perfect voice control, but perfect body control as well. He said we should learn this art from the circus performers whose every leap was not only bold, but justified as well.

Sometimes. when watching an unsuccessful performance, he would repeat Goethe's remark on the theatre: "I would like the stage to be as narrow as the rope of a rope-walker: this would discourage many untalented persons from choosing it as their career."

These were not empty words. During rehearsals of Donani's pantomime, Lecocq's comic operas and *Day and Night,* the stage became a circus ring. Professional acrobats and jugglers would teach the actors their tricks. Later, when we were rehearsing *Romeo and Juliet,* we watched a circus performer patiently teach our young Romeo how to climb a rope-ladder gracefully to Juliet's balcony. The circus touches that Tairov used with such imagination did much to enrich our performances.

As the years passed I became more and more enamoured of the circus. I never missed an opportunity to see a performance, either at home or abroad. During one of our foreign tours I was indeed fortunate to see the magnificent clown Grok.

I still follow the careers of Soviet circus performers closely, for they represent the most courageous and beautiful of all arts.

1963

MOSCOW IN FLAMES

(V. Mayakovsky and the Circus)

By A. Fevralsky

Mayakovsky wrote *Moscow in Flames* especially for the circus, to commemorate the 25th anniversary of the 1905 Revolution. The original title was *1905*.

The first part of the presentation was based on the Manifesto of October 17. a general strike, preparations for an armed uprising, fighting on the barricades, a punitive expedition and the defeat of revolutionary Presnya. Mayakovsky said his intention was to present "a general idea of 1905" in which the audience would see how "the working class went through its dress rehearsal, and to bring events up-to-date."

These recollections of 1905 stressed their continuity and their relationship to current events.

When Mayakovsky began working on *Moscow in Flames* he made a thorough study of everything pertaining to the events of the first Russian revolution and used these data in his presentation. including satirical poems and songs of the period and several comic skits based on political cartoons of the time.

Moscow in Flames was more of a review than even *Mystery-Buff*. Its twenty-odd episodes included a great number of characters, most of whom appeared only once. Thus it was, according to Mayakovsky, "a literary and historical arrangement." The sequence of scenes was

In the "Moscow in Flames" panto-mime, the circus experimented with historical themes

determined by the chronology of actual events. Thus, as a whole, it was a panorama of the 1905 Revolution as seen from the vantage point of the Soviet epoch.

As in *Mystery-Buff*, the emotional impact of the play was largely determined by a masterly combination of comedy, buffoonery and drama.

Moscow in Flames was, of all Mayakovsky's work, most akin to *Mystery-Buff* in its manner of presenting a mass popular spectacle, in its scope, exaggeration, its simple language intended for a large auditorium and sharpened to a fine point by the magnificent poetry which took it from the heights of true publicism to a level of somewhat crude, satiric humour. Though the "cosmic" scale of *Mystery-Buff* was absent in *Moscow in Flames,* the scene was now the country as a whole, now a great metropolis, and the words from "Order to the Army of Art" came to life anew:

> *The streets—our hands,*
> *The square—our easel...*

Mayakovsky's emergence as the author of a major work written especially for the circus was in no way accidental. It was the logical conclusion of everything he had done before as a dramatist. In *Mystery-Buff, The Bedbug,* and *The Bath-House* circus tricks and magic were included in plays to be presented in the theatre, as noted in the subtitles of the latter two: "A Magic Comedy" and "A Drama with a Circus and Fireworks," while several scenes from *Mystery-Buff* were rehearsed in the circus. *The Championship of the World Class Struggle* which appeared later and was written especially for the circus was a short production with only three circus acts—wrestling, clowning and a monologue. *Moscow in Flames,* the last of these, was truly a circus spectacular, including every kind of genre possible beneath the Big Top.

Mayakovsky enriched the circus with his political awareness and wit, with his magnificent poetry and sense of drama. However, *Moscow in Flames* was in no way an experiment in producing drama in the circus. Mayakovsky's script was based on the very specific nature of the circus, in many episodes the playwright and master of the written word stepped aside for the playwright producer of spectacles. It is in the various remarks and marginal notations of *Moscow in Flames* that we find a new aspect of Mayakovsky, the playwright. Though Mayakovsky always took part in staging his plays, never before had he risen to his full height as a producer. We find in the marginal notes uncommon imagination and wit in staging the action and situation comedy. Mayakovsky made extremely good use of the various circus genres and of the different means necessary to produce the desired effect. His working copy contains such precise and definite descriptions of the clowning, traditional circus tricks and acts, and of the accessories used, that the producer finds he has little to do—everything has already been done for him by the author.

There is a red-headed clown and one who plays a musical instrument, there are other clowns, a trapeze act, aerialists, a stilt-walker, various parades, animal-trainers with hoops, horses, dogs and an aquatic pantomime, and all this is part and parcel of the theme, each act or trick serves to emphasise a given event or characterise a given personage. Thus, the red-headed clown jumping through a hoop personified Kerensky's career as a minister, etc. Mayakovsky said: "The circus today is beginning to drift away from naked tricks in an attempt to present the various acts in some social content. Thus, water fulfils a very special role of its own, washing away fences. The same is true of the horses."

All available space was to be used, the ring, the barrier, the specially built platforms and the entire area within the circus. Lighting played a great part in changing scenes, in spotlighting groups of performers. There were numbers that shone in the dark, rays of light, a map that lit up, and a shining hammer and sickle that rose from the water. A screen was used for producing shadows and showing excerpts from films.

The dialogue followed the traditional circus plan.

It was only in the Heralds' Introduction that the text was of a generalised nature. Otherwise, the dialogue followed the action. Both were like a series of posters, short and to the point. That is why it fitted in so well in a theatre in the round, that is why it did not detract from the circus acts but provided extra emphasis. The overall effect of the spoken parts was heightened by frequent changes in rhythm and inflexion. Thus, the Prologue recited by the heralds began with the solemn appeal:

> Proud of the year 1917,
> Don't forget about 1905!
> A year of undying glory and fame,
> When the dream of the land came alive...

and was followed by a scene that began with a clown's comic query:

What for such a dreadful amount of pants?

This scene was an image created with words and put into action. The same principle was used in several other scenes as, for instance, the bloody paw that appeared through the tsar's manifesto.

The circus arena gave Mayakovsky an opportunity to present spectacular scenes which could only be hinted at on a regular stage: a fire, barricade battles, a cavalry charge, horse-drawn carriages and trams, automobiles and tractors. Of special interest was the magnificent caricature of the dethroned dynasty in which equestrian and larger-than-life statues of former tsars came forth and broke ranks as a clown standing on a shattered crown recited:

Comrade circus, where's your grin?
Here's a sight to tickle us:
Look and see who's trotting in:
The dynasty of Nicholas!

Despite its great diversity of theatrical effects, *Moscow in Flames* was staged according to a single artistic principle. To this day it remains the only major literary work written especially for the circus.

1940

Vsevolod Meyerhold, an outstanding stage director, became interested in the circus in pre-revolutionary times, seeing it as a school of good health and courage. This interest increased after the October Revolution, when new horizons opened up before Soviet art.

"We, the workers of all fields of art, the theatre and the circus must join forces in our common task and, with as much unity of opinion as possible, bring our art to the people," Meyerhold said in 1918.

Meyerhold was named head of the Petrograd division of the Theatrical Department of the People's Commissariat of Education that same year. He visualised the new challenge to the circus thus: "The circus is a house in which the art of physical education, of physical beauty, will rise ever higher. The new circus studios will train instructors who will then travel to various parts of the country to create new sports clubs and a new physical culture, for a healthy body means a healthy spirit."

Meyerhold did not regard the circus merely as a school of physical education. He saw both its artistic side and the possibility of establishing close relations between it and the theatre. He said that "there is no true dividing line between the circus and the theatre, you can find the theatre in the circus, while the circus strives to bring its charms to the theatre. Stage directors and producers are called upon to reform circus productions.

"But the circus should not change at anyone's say-so. The reform must come from within the circus itself, it must be carried out by the circus performers, for there is no such a thing as a theatre-circus and there should not be, but each is and should be an entity in itself, each with its own laws and structure.

"True, the theatre and variety shows, by supplying elements of their own art to the circus, have done it much harm and still continue to harm the development of a circus art *per se*. True, during the most theatrical of all theatrical epochs the circus had a definite influence on the development of theatrical art *per se* (and especially so in Japan and Italy). Nevertheless, in contemplating a reform of the circus and the theatre, conditions must be created under which both will develop along parallel, not crossing lines."

Meyerhold went on to say that actors had much to learn from the circus (acrobatics, for instance), basing his observations on the fact that beginning with the late 19th century the theatre had gone into decline. He dreamed of creating an acrobatic secondary school. The boys and girls who graduated from this school, would be healthy, vivacious, lithe, ready to go into the circus or the theatre, to choose comedy, tragedy or drama, as their life's work. He felt that a revival of a theatrical culture with actors who had perfect body control was one of the roads leading to the creation of a theatre that could cope with the complex tasks set it by the Revolution. Meyerhold tried to put this theory into practice in his work as a pedagogue and producer.

In 1920, the R.S.F.S.R. Theatre-I opened in Moscow with Meyerhold as its director. Mayakovsky's *Mystery-Buff* was the second play they staged. Meyerhold and Bebutov, the two directors, introduced several circus skits in the play, which was wholly in keeping with its popular, heroic and satirical nature. Thus, the Agreer (with an excellent performance by Igor

You can see how well Meyerhold's production reflects the circus atmosphere

Ilyinsky) was a barely concealed circus clown. The Devils that appeared in the Third Act ("Hell") were presented in the same vein. Besides, an entire circus act was included, with Vitaly Lazarenko, a popular circus performer, climbing down a rope from the ceiling, doing various tricks as he descended. We find the following excerpt in the memoirs of Valery Sysoyev, The Man of the Future in the play.

Lazarenko, illuminated by a red spotlight, did very dangerous tricks on a trapeze. For instance, he would sit swinging on it, waving his arms about, and then suddenly plunge headlong towards the stage, grasping the corners of the trapeze with his toes at the very last moment.

Meyerhold made use of circus and popular comedy in his production of A. Sukhovo-Kobylin's *The Death of Tarelkin,* which the author intended as a farce and grotesque and which was quite eccentric on the whole. There was a generous helping of slapstick comedy, with the gloomy world of tsarist officialdom and police precincts presented in such a grotesque manner as to parody the whole. The settings were in keeping with the spirit of the play, and each prop had something wrong with it: the chair seats would suddenly fall out, backs would fall off, a footstool backfired, the legs of a table slid in opposite directions, sending it crashing to the floor, only to rally and become its former reliable self again. This mass of tricks in no way interfered with the actors, who brought every word of the magnificent text home to the audience.

Sergei Eisenstein, then studying under Meyerhold, was his assistant producer for the play. At the end of the season both Eisenstein and Meyerhold put on two independent and very different productions of Ostrovsky's *There's Enough Simplicity to Every Wise Man,* making use of various circus tricks in both productions. Unlike *The Death of Tarelkin,* staged by Meyerhold in strict accordance with the author's text, the play staged by Eisenstein was first completely rewritten by him and Sergei Tretyakov, the result being a topical political review presented as a circus spectacle. The printed programme carried out the same theme with the words "Working in the ring are..." instead of the usual "List of Characters."

An actor emotes

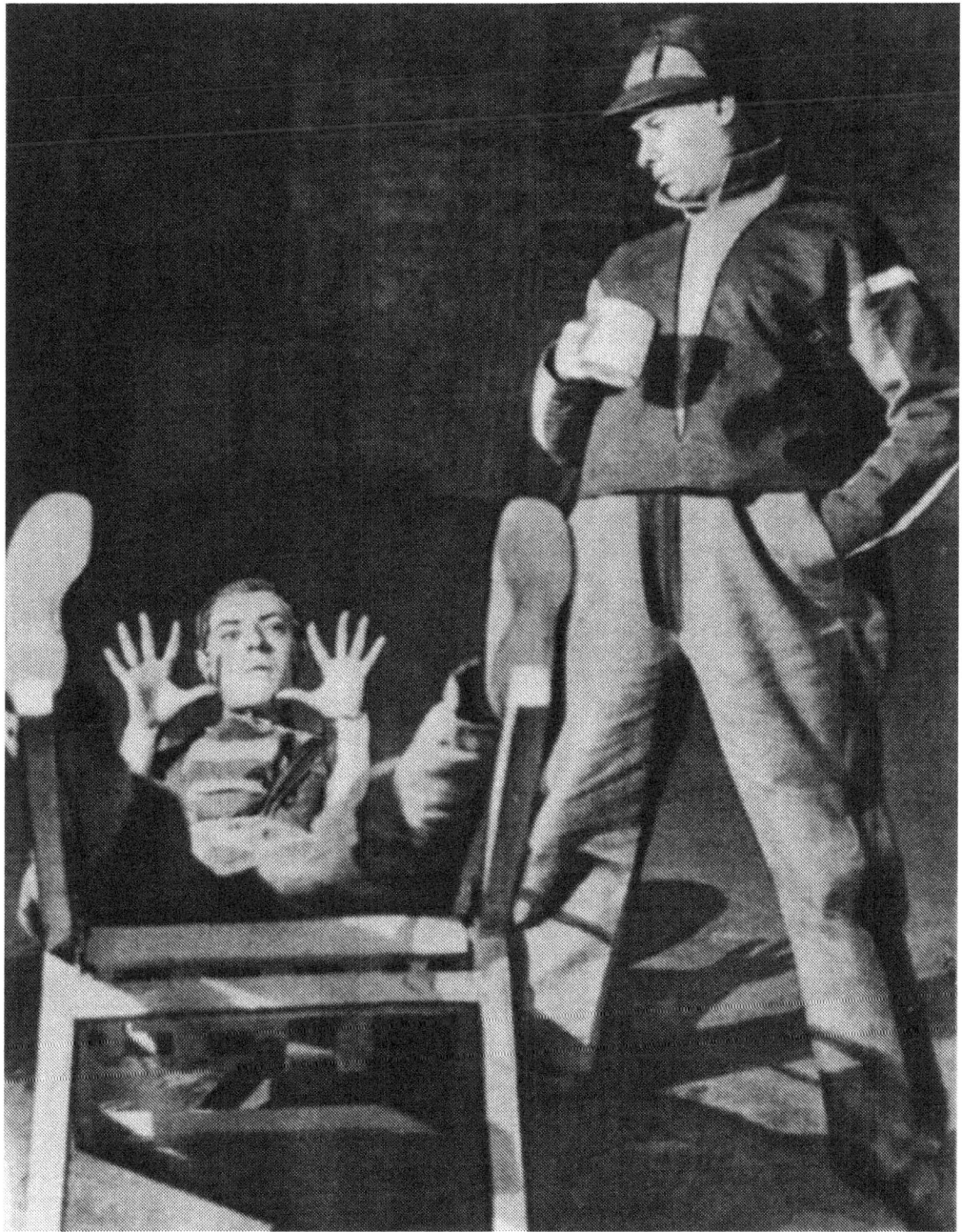

Mayakovsky's play *The Bath-House,* presented in 1930, has the following subtitle: "A Drama in Six Acts with a Circus and Fireworks." Using this as his guide, Meyerhold injected a carnival spirit into the play. Thus, Pobedonosikov appears as a grotesque, ridiculous clown, with Maxim Shtraukh playing an unforgettable Pobedonosikov.

Several of Meyerhold's pupils worked in the circus, as did Nikolai Ekk, who later became a well-known film producer. It was he who staged the mass circus spectacular *To October, From Us* at the Moscow Circus in 1927. The script was written by Nazim Hikmet, who lived in Moscow from 1922 to 1928, in collaboration with Regina Yanushkevich, an actress and playwright and one of Meyerhold's pupils. This was to be a show for children, re-creating the events of the October Revolution and the first ten years of Soviet power. Circus performers, actors and amateur groups took part in what was one of the first mass presentations in the history of the Soviet circus based on a contemporary political theme.

Three of Meyerhold's former pupils were producers at the Moscow Circus in the years following the Second World War. These were Nikolai Basilov, Alexander Zaikov and Mark Mestechkin. The knowledge and skills they acquired from their teacher, Vsevolod Meyerhold, has done much to enrich their work in the circus arena.

1963

SERGEI EISENSTEIN'S CIRCUS PROJECTS

By Y. Krasovsky

The scene was Moscow, 1922. The Civil War had just ended, leaving in its wake destruction, poverty and hunger. But in the country that had already begun to reconstruct, there was a turbulent blossoming of a new, revolutionary culture, and young writers, artists and actors now came to the forefront.

This was also a time of heated discussions.

Young Mayakovsky was a new and powerful voice to be contended with, Meyerhold was passionately defending his "Theatrical October," the biting political fables of Demyan Bedny were being quoted everywhere and Lunacharsky discussed literature and art with great knowledge and conviction.

And then, among the noisy, many-voiced crowd of enthusiasts and innovators in art at the Morozov Mansion (now Friendship House), there appeared a curly-haired twenty-four-year-old artist and producer who had just been demobilised from the Red Army. His name was Sergei Eisenstein. Grigory Alexandrov and Maxim Shtraukh, the two youths who always accompanied him, were just as enthusiastic about art as he was. They, too, dreamed of a "new word" in art. Eisenstein and the playwright S. Tretyakov decided to produce Ostrovsky's play *There's Enough Simplicity to Every Wise*

Man, but all that was left of the original when they got through with it was the title and the names of several of the characters.

Eisenstein described his efforts in editing Ostrovsky in an article written in 1928: "My aim was to achieve a revolutionary modernisation of Ostrovsky, i.e., a social re-evaluation of his characters, seeing them as they might appear today."

Indeed, the result was an eccentric theatrical presentation, no more, with Ostrovsky as the starting point. It was during this period that Eisenstein, seeking new roads in art, created his "attraction" theory. The essence of this theory (which he was to later refute) was the concept that a theatrical presentation should be a loosely strung series of individual emotional experiences or "attractions," with a powerful political theme as its basis.

The use of the word "attraction" was intended. There were many circus touches in Eisenstein's *Wise Man*. He defended this innovation in an article written in 1923: "The cinema is the school of film editing, as is, most notably, the music hall and circus. To put it plainly, to produce a good play you must first put together a good music hall or circus programme with the theme of the play as your starting point."

The Wise Man had rope-walking, acrobatics done on a pole, triple somersaults on an imaginary horse and clowning in every shape and form. If one were to judge the performance as an experimental circus review and not from the point of view of the obviously faulty "attraction" theory, it was undoubtedly worthy of interest.

The Wise Man was presented in the Great Hall of the Morozov Mansion. A tight-wire was strung at an angle from the floor to the sculptured cornice and a "Man in a Mask" walked down the wire. The man of mystery was played by G. Alexandrov, who later produced *Jolly Fellows* and *Circus*, two all-time favourite Soviet films. V. Yanukova did acrobatics on a pole high above the floor, while M. Shtraukh and I. Pyryev, both future People's Artistes of the U.S.S.R., performed below ("in the ring," according to the printed programme).

We find the following lines in Sergei Eisenstein's unpublished memoirs: "I have loved clowns since infancy and have always felt a bit ashamed of this.

"Father also loved the circus, but he was most impressed with championship riding and Williams Trucci's trained horses.

232

I did my best to conceal my passion for the clowns and made-believe I, too, was terribly interested in the horses!

"I had my sweet revenge in 1922, when I literally 'flooded' my first independent production (*The Wise Man*) with every shade and colour of circus clowns and straight men.

"Mamma Glumova—clown

"Glumov—straight man

"Krutitsky—straight man

"Mamayev—straight man

"All the servants—clowns

"Turusina—clown

"Gorodulin (played by Pyryev) was worth three clowns!"

According to P. Atasheva, Eisenstein's wife, he remained an avid circus fan long after his childhood and youth were over, seeing the circus as an optimistic, joyous form of art.

Ten years passed. Eisenstein, now a world-famous producer, once again turned to the circus for his theme. We find in his archives the manuscript of a political circus review entitled *The Hand of Moscow*, which had apparently been written in 1932.

Following is an excerpt from the Introduction.

"The performance consists of a series of episodes which describe the fifteen years that have elapsed since the October Revolution. The first point of departure is the Armistice and the Versailles Peace Treaty. The Brest Peace Treaty is the second point of departure.

"List of Characters:

"A Guide—who accompanies a foreign tourist and recounts the history of the past years from the point of view of a complaining sceptic and alarmist. The action constantly contradicts his dire prophecies.

"The Newborn World—'Baby'—symbolising Versailles, a bloodthirsty soldier, the embodiment of 'War.'

"'Daddy'—a character that never appears on stage, but dictates its will to 'Baby's' educators, godfathers and guardians. 'Daddy' symbolises capitalism.

"Portraits of and satires on personages known to the world during the past fifteen years,

"Allegorical beasts symbolising the governments of various nations."

There follows a detailed development of the theme. On the one hand, there were the heroic events of the Revolution and life in a new Russia; on the other, there was a biting, satirical description of the capitalist world, of the enemies of the young Soviet Republic. The scene changes from the front-lines to Versailles, to the workers' quarters. Passing in review are the major international events of the preceding fifteen years. The review ends with a recital in verse of the Five Year Plan and a "parade of socialism in construction."

This, naturally, was just a draft. The actual review seemed very promising. This original, contemporary political review was to have been produced in the circus. One can only regret that Sergei Eisenstein, that great master, connoisseur and lover of the circus, never realised this project.

1960

www.ingramcontent.com/pod-product-compliance
Lightning Source LLC
Chambersburg PA
CBHW081326090426
42737CB00017B/3043

9 781589 639706